RECALIBRATE
Real People in Gig Harbor Changing Course

Table of Contents

DEDICATION

Dedicated to all the people of Gig Harbor who
recalibrate, courageously choosing to risk
changing the course of their lives.

The book you are about to read
is a compilation of authentic life stories.
The facts are true, and the events are real.
These storytellers have dealt with crisis, tragedy, abuse
and neglect and have shared their most private moments,
mess-ups and hang-ups in order for others to learn and
grow from them. In order to protect the identities of those
involved in their pasts, the names and details of some
storytellers have been withheld or changed.

INTRODUCTION

"Sometimes you will never know the value of a moment until it becomes a memory." *– Dr. Seuss*

Some would say life is a series of moments. When strung together, they say something about you and your story, which is defined by the sum of these moments — both the good and the bad. Some you hoped would never end, and others you wish you could have back. They may have happened to you or as a result of the choices you made.

What happens when you are left disappointed and disillusioned? Maybe your life is nowhere near where you had imagined. What do you do? What if your life could be different? Would you take advantage of that opportunity? Or would you allow it to pass you by?

We invite you to read the following stories and to see how real people in Gig Harbor took the risk and chose to change their course. And change their destinies.

BREAKING THE SHELL
The Story of Kyle
Written by Mike Ward

"Kids, Mom is sick."

My younger sister and I glanced at each other. She tilted her head and looked up at Dad.

"What does she have?" Taylor asked. "The flu?"

"No," Dad said. His face told us what, at age 9, I wasn't ready to hear.

❧❧❧

Born in California, I spent my earliest years in Redwood City.

Dad put his art to the side for a nine-to-five job at a bank, while Mom made Betty Crocker proud. Mom cooked, cleaned and watched out for us as kids.

At 4 years old, I had my daily gear. My backpack was stocked with gadgets, action figures and snacks (gadgets typically meant more action figures). Prepared to hike across the Wild West, forge through the Amazon or make a brave last stand against the "bad guys" at any moment, I never struggled to find adventure.

Only a year and a half younger, my sister, Taylor, grew into a stark contrast of my personality. While I quietly daydreamed, she exuded natural extroversion.

One day, when I was 6, Mom and Dad called to my

sister and me, "Kyle and Taylor! Come here, please." My mother's voice carried through the house like honey.

"What? What's going on? Kyle did it!" Taylor tumbled into the room.

I quietly walked into the room, half lost in a distant imaginary galaxy.

"Calm down, Taylor. No one did anything wrong. Grandpa is sick, so we're moving to Washington to help take care of him."

And so we made our move to Gig Harbor, Washington.

Arriving at our new house, my sister and I ran off to play in the woods. We came back to a modest, cozy home, nestled in the tree line. Juniper trees with long sweeping leaves welcomed us onto the front porch. The sunset sprinkling through the tree branches captured the world in a warm glow.

Grandpa fought hard. He eventually recovered, and the doctors cleared him of cancer. We remained in Gig Harbor.

❧❧❧

"Kids, this summer you are going to stay at your aunt's house."

The infinite possibilities of elementary-school summer surged through me.

"I get to spend the whole summer in California?" I double-checked the exciting news.

BREAKING THE SHELL

"Yes, Kyle. And I expect you to watch after your sister, too."

"DAD," Taylor protested. "I'm 7 and a half. I can watch after myself!"

We packed the car and left for a gorgeous summer vacation. My biggest concerns that summer were choosing my destination to explore on a given day and determining how much I could fit into my backpack.

That was the last time I indulged in the bliss of childhood.

ॐॐॐ

"Kyle and Taylor, could you please come out to the porch?"

Something did not feel right.

"I need to speak with you two."

I stepped out onto the porch. The Washington forest air greeted me like a damp blanket. I quietly sat down on the porch with my sister. I glanced at the pine trees in the front yard.

"Kids, Mom is sick. She has been in treatment over the summer."

"What does she have? The flu?" I could feel Taylor fidgeting next to me.

"She has a type of cancer called *melanoma*."

I stared off into the juniper bushes.

Taylor pried, still piecing things together, "When will she be okay?"

"It doesn't look like she will be getting better, kids."

The long green pines bent lightly in the wind.

"Your mother will be staying in the hospital for treatment."

At 9 years old, I could not make much sense of this.

I bet pine trees don't ever get melanoma.

Mom stayed at the hospital in Tacoma, 20 minutes from Gig Harbor. We started packing up Dad's '89 Volvo wagon to go visit Mom regularly.

I typically stared out the window at the hospital as we arrived. It looked like a giant spaceship. Coming from our home in the forest to a sterilized environment, the masks, scrubs and equipment everywhere only perpetuated the foreign feeling of the hospital.

I would stare out of the window and watch the city of Tacoma go about its business while time seemed to stop inside Mom's room.

"Kyle?"

"Hmm?"

"I asked you how school was, sweetheart?"

"Oh, it was good."

She smiled.

It wasn't easy for anyone. She handled herself with such grace and strength, and we were always happy to see her. But I could not deal with the frustration, confusion and anger of losing my mom. Life felt so chaotic. I craved a neat, organized life. I spent a lot of time in my imagination, leaving reality behind. It became harder when I could not ignore that she'd lost her beautiful hair, when she began to look pale and thin.

My imagination did not block out the fact that my mother could no longer take care of me, and I'd have to take care of her.

These things take time to get a grasp on, but watching my mother fade in the hospital, it became obvious that time was something we did not have.

She spared none. The situation slowly drifted from the hope of recovery, then settled into a hope to die in a comfortable, loving environment. She made the decision to leave the hospital and spend her remaining days in our home.

We cleared out the living room and put a bed in the center. We moved everything out except for the vibrant orchids that my grandfather taught my dad to appreciate and cultivate.

Mom spent her final days in that room. I never gave up. I knew what the doctors said, but even if I heard it said 100 times, I refused to believe it. Death was such an incomprehensibly definite experience, and my heart could not accept it, no matter how many times my brain heard it.

One day, Dad called us in to sit down. His face already said the words I could not stand to hear.

"Your mother … has passed."

Silence consumed the room. Sunlight glowed through the windows, and an orange hue contrasted my father's dim orchids. The three of us cried at her bedside. The presence of my mother disappeared and left a void in the room. The heaviness of pain quickly pressed in. I do not know how long we sat there, but eventually someone entered the room and interrupted our silence.

In the following weeks, it seemed like I had a "free hugs" sign around my neck. Every teacher in school would stop to give me a hug. I did not fight it. I needed it.

My father became distant. He grieved Mom's death in his own way. He built a wall that effectively kept everyone out, and unfortunately that included my sister and me. Taylor isolated herself as well, in just as much confusion as my father.

Nobody could possibly relate to my loss. When I returned to school, my friends were still worried about their latest homework assignment. I wanted to be worried about my homework assignment so bad. I often felt alone in the world, but those hugs I received could so easily shatter my delusion, if only for a moment.

ॐॐॐ

"You're not even my *real* mom! AND YOU NEVER WILL BE!" Taylor spat at our new stepmom, Julie.

"Taylor, I'm not trying to replace your mother! I just need you to show me some respect!"

"Well, I don't respect you! And I don't *have* to listen to you, either."

The door served as a barrier from watching them argue. As long as I stayed in my room, I could hide. But the noise had no problem strolling right through my door. Not even a slight muffle.

BREAKING THE SHELL

I buried myself in my schoolwork, hoping to escape my new house altogether.

Dad and Julie replaced everything. No more beat-up cars or small house in the forest. Cookie-cutter suburban dream homes packed our new neighborhood with the proverbial 1.5 nice cars in the driveway, 2.5 kids and a white picket fence. I quickly acquainted myself with a suburban lifestyle. With big houses in every direction, I could no longer wander off into the forest, so I had to find a new means of escape. I spent hours on homework, the new Nintendo 64, and often walked outside of our picket fence to visit a friend's home.

Mom had only passed the year before, and Dad had already remarried. Julie was nice. I never had a problem with her — I wanted my father to be happy, and she made him happy. I could see that, but Taylor never really accepted it.

Taylor, being the natural extrovert, never had a problem voicing her opinion.

Julie had two children of her own. I remember them being so much younger, even though I was only a few years older at the ripe old age of 10. Maybe they were just more innocent. They were still children.

During the next few years, my neighbor Craig became my best friend.

"Kyle, with all of the time you spend here, I think I can claim you on my taxes!" Craig's mother smiled at me, not realizing my desire to move out of my own home.

One day, Dad and Julie called Taylor into the living

room to talk. As my sister walked by my room, I could see the self-inflicted scars on her arms.

I did not hear much, other than Dad telling Taylor that she would be leaving.

I thought Julie saw Taylor as a problem and that she'd resolved to get rid of the problem. Without much of a choice, Taylor packed up and moved to our aunt's in California.

Taylor's absence did nothing to lighten the mood at home. My father and stepmom argued heatedly.

Fortunately, as I progressed in school, it became easier to remain busy with homework.

When I began high school, I started going to school across the street. I could conveniently study there after school, and when I left the school building, I could stay at Craig's house next door. I found a job at a grocery store and began saving up for a car. The only thing that stopped me from spending even more time at work was a state law that prohibited any student under 18 from working more than 20 hours per week.

ৡৡৡ

"Hey, Kyle, will you pass the chips?" Craig called to me without looking away from his computer screen.

At 2 a.m., chips were a vital source of fuel in order to continue our computer game marathon.

"Yeah, Ladies' Man. Quit hogging the chips!" Andrew risked looking away from his screen and punched me in the shoulder, laughing.

BREAKING THE SHELL

Ladies' Man proved a not-so-difficult nickname to acquire, considering the present company. My group of friends gathered regularly to spend the night playing StarCraft in someone's basement. We called that a party.

Ladies' Man.

I could get a phone number and take a girl out.

I saved up money, bought a car and ranked in the top of my class at school. My life looked good — from the outside.

I received praise from my managers and teachers alike, and I had the girls, the car, the friends.

None of it mattered.

All of the extra hours at school, all of the time at work, every moment working on my car and every night with my friends all served as an escape from my house.

As long as I was not home, I didn't have to listen to Julie and my dad yell at each other.

I didn't have to wonder about Taylor. Dad seemed so lost on how to handle Taylor. I still blamed Julie for forcing her out to avoid the problem altogether, but Taylor's absence only caused problems to show up everywhere else. Dad could only sleep in the guest room so many times before it became apparent to me that they were headed for a divorce. I wanted nothing to do with any of it.

I did not know what a good relationship actually looked like. I just needed distraction. So in that sense, girlfriends were essentially another car to work on, job to put extra hours into or an essay to write for class.

Relationships became more physical, and I thought I had found a new solution to my loneliness.

Like with all of the other temporary solutions I found, the void inside never really filled.

Everything looked great on the outside, and I had it all together. But inside I remained scared, confused and lost.

のかのか

"Dad! What are you doing here? You shouldn't be shopping at this grocery store, this is the expensive grocery store!" The tone in my voice matched the concern in my eyes. I knew he could not afford to shop where I worked.

"Kyle, calm down. Something came in the mail today. I thought you might want to open it."

I looked down, and he handed me an envelope.

University of Idaho.

I opened the letter, and we read it together.

"Congratulations …"

Dad hugged me. "I'm so happy for you, Kyle. I love you. You deserve this."

I could go off to college. I could start entirely fresh. Nobody knew me, and I could be whoever I wanted to. This would make everything better.

のかのか

"Welcome to your University of Idaho tour!" Luke smiled.

"What are you going to study?" He went around the room asking each person.

"Well, I'm thinking of going into mathematics or maybe music. I'm not quite sure," one of the other kids replied.

My dad leaned over and whispered something to me. "Sounds like community college to me," he cracked with a grin.

I chuckled. Luke made his way to me.

"How about you? What will you study?"

With precisely no hesitation, I replied, "Chemical Engineering."

"Wow, that's tough. Are you sure?"

"Yes. I'm going to graduate with a degree in chemical engineering." I knew what I wanted, and I knew how to get it. I always had. I knew how to get the car, the money, the friends and the girl. Nothing had stopped me before, and I knew I could do it.

The summer before I left for college, Dad and Julie split. We moved into a small home in rural Gig Harbor, and Taylor spent weeks at a time living with her friends. Dad barely covered bills with his pay as a part-time art teacher.

I spent the whole summer fantasizing about starting fresh in the fall. Nobody knew my identity, and I could be whoever I wanted to be. I showed little care for my family. I just wanted to leave — anything was better than home.

RECALIBRATE

😂😂😂

Dad and I pulled up to the freshman dorm. The leaves fell in a colored chaos, similar to the visual chaos of masses of people scrambling around. Parents made small talk with one another and helped get their kids moved in.

Older students helped everyone get settled. They seemed to be the only people there who didn't resemble ants running around. The only ones who knew what they were doing.

I caught the eye of Luke, who had run my campus tour the previous spring.

Without skipping a beat, he walked up to my father and me. "Hey, guys! It's good to see you again. Can I help you with anything?" He greeted us with a warm smile

My father and I were both a little surprised that he recognized us so easily.

"Well, we could use some help with the bags —" my father started.

"Sure. No problem!"

I noticed the subtle shift in Dad's eyebrows from surprised to suspicious.

Luke and my dad chatted throughout the whole process. Suspicious or not, we were happy to have the help. Luke showed us which lines to get in and how to get through the whole process as quickly as possible, then proceeded to help carry everything to my room with us.

Luke invited me to a barbeque later. Some freshmen relished the opportunity to make friends at a college party.

As the guy who'd already budgeted out my entire semester, my motivation was the free food.

හංහංහං

Luke picked me up in his gold '80s Buick. He drove it like a hotrod.

I'll admit the barbeque wasn't quite what I'd expected. Around the time they finished prepping the food, I realized a couple things. Everyone drank water or soda and smiled a whole bunch. Then they did something I hadn't expected.

Everybody gathered around the food and began to pray.

What have I gotten myself into?

I had no experience with religion growing up, and it did not fit into my curriculum for chemical engineering.

I took some time to think about the situation. There I stood, a guy who never drank in high school, worked hard, studied and turned my homework in on time. After a quick cost-benefit analysis, I realized that my lifestyle held many similarities to Luke's in all of those regards, so it would not be so hard to keep hanging around him. And the free food didn't hurt.

These guys didn't know me — I had my chance to build a new identity.

හංහංහං

Jacob paused between tacos at Taco Time. "You don't look too hot, Kyle."

"Yeah, I'm not feeling too well."

"Have you gone to the doctor?" all of the guys inquired in unison.

"No, I've been busy."

Jacob looked at me, grabbed a napkin and held it up to me. "Blow your nose in this."

I took the napkin, blew my nose and began to throw it away when he grabbed it from me and opened it up. The off-colored mucus isn't something I'd have inspected at the table, but none of the guys seemed to mind.

"We're taking you to the doctor."

Those were the kind of guys I had been hanging around my first couple months of school.

I found them strange. I grew up seeking ways to escape loneliness and fear, so it became second nature for me to use people as distractions. My friends, girlfriends, teachers, bosses, all in the past became objects that I could use for my own selfish gains, whether it be money, emotions or praise.

Luke, Jacob and the other guys acted unlike anyone I knew. They *wanted* to go out of their way to help me.

When they invited me to attend a Bible study each week, another quick cost-benefit analysis made that one an easy choice.

For years I worked to get my praise. In every area of my life, I knew to work hard, show value and gain respect. Soon I noticed that these friendships were different. The guys would come by and make sure I took breaks from studying.

One day Zach, one of the guys from our Bible study, knocked at my door.

"Hey, Kyle, you missed Bible study tonight."

"Yeah, I know ... I just ..."

"You don't need to explain, man. I just wanted to make sure you are okay."

I started to realize that they didn't just want to help me — they *cared* about me.

I hadn't had anyone comfort me that way since my mother got sick.

These guys seemed a little kooky. They valued me as a friend but made it very clear that my value stemmed from nothing I had done. I could not earn their respect, they just gave it to me.

I tried to do whatever they did, thinking that would encourage them to continue treating me with such kindness and concern. I bought a Bible, I raised my hands during worship and I would clap at the right time in the songs.

Once again, I seemed to fit in — from all outward appearances. These guys thought I was great!

There remained one problem: I could not figure out why I never felt happy. I smiled like I saw them smiling, and I showed them a happy, willing side of me that they all seemed to love, but it merely covered my inner self like a thin, fragile eggshell. Inside I felt like a delicate, fear-driven, lonely kid.

RECALIBRATE

During one of our weekend camps, I sensed God might be speaking to me.

In dew-covered grass, I overlooked a river where the morning mist began to recede as the sun burned it away. I sat cross-legged and quiet, like I had seen others do while meditating. Then I saw an image.

I saw the faces of Luke, Jacob and Zach. The vision compelled me to get closer to those guys. For the first time, I felt like I believed.

Immediately afterward, I excitedly shared this vision with everyone at the camp. I had heard people speak of such things and how great it sounded. I shared my vision as an investment in the identity I had built up. I could act nice, show concern, jump during worship, and now I had a vision to share.

Man, it was easy to be a Christian!

ᐒᐒᐒ

Jacob pulled me aside before I could even greet him. "Hey, Kyle, I want to talk with you about something."

"Okaaaay." I hesitated as we walked into a separate room in the church. I looked around the room clearly built in the '80s and saw Luke, Jacob and Zach. I had never been so uncomfortable on a shag carpet.

Did I do something wrong? What if they know that I have been faking this?

Jacob broke the silence.

"So I was thinking about what you shared at camp last week."

In a nervous glance, I looked over to Luke. He did not hesitate to continue where Jacob left off. "Have you actually turned your life over to Jesus?"

"What do you mean?"

Zach said in a soft tone, "You talk like us, you sing like us, you even journal and read your Bible, Kyle. But have you made a commitment to legitimately dedicate yourself to Christ? If not, it's almost like you are just playing the part."

The jig is up. They've seen right through my façade.

"No," I said to the shag carpet.

I felt my persona break. *They're going to ask me to leave.*

I expected rejection. I readied myself to be shamed.

I never expected what came next.

Luke smiled. "Well, let's make it right."

I prayed to receive Christ, and then they each prayed over me. The image I'd tried to project shattered, but not because I messed up. The image shattered because, after that, it became real. Instead of just doing this to fit in, I made a decision to do this for God.

My life from there changed beyond what I can describe. A personal relationship with a loving God was something I had heard about 100 times, but never realized that I didn't understand. After that prayer, I felt like I truly *knew*. He resided there, in my heart.

"Guys, I thought you were going to be mad at me," I admitted.

"Kyle, we just want you to have a genuine relationship with Jesus. But we love you, no matter what."

No matter what. I didn't have to prove anything to these guys. The love they showed was an attempt to share the love of God. I couldn't believe I actually had a personal relationship with that God.

ॐ ॐ ॐ

The window looked the same as it had the prior week. I studied that window. Not intentionally, but as my last year in college came to an end, I'd applied for countless jobs without a single offer. I'd recently picked up a new hobby — staring out windows and wondering what would happen in my future.

My instinct said to fight for what I needed. If I just worked harder at finding a job, I could make it happen. However, having tried that already, it felt more like a fish out of water trying to jump higher. Even if I jumped higher, I would still come back down on dry land. So I took a different approach.

"God, I don't know what I am supposed to do, but please show me. I need your help."

Not long after, the message came through, loud and clear.

Stay.

So I decided to listen. I was going to get my degree in a

month with no job lined up and no idea what to do, but I trusted that God had a plan for me.

That week, I bumped into a professor for whom I had worked in the summer.

"Hey, Kyle! It's good to see you."

"Good to see you, too, Professor. How are you?"

"I am well. Come to think of it, I wanted to chat with you."

"Sure, what's up?"

"I was wondering — would you be interested in being a research assistant for me? Your graduate degree would be paid for in full, and you would be paid monthly on top of that."

It did not matter how many jobs I applied to, I realized. God opened a door for me that I did not even know was there. I simply had to trust in him.

ર્જાર્જાર્જા

As I was finishing up my graduate degree, I felt God telling me to leave. Job offers emerged, and the University of Idaho campus ministry seemed to be in good hands as new leaders were stepping up. I did not know where to go, but I wanted to listen to God.

One day, my cell phone rang. It was Taylor.

"Kyle, I need to tell you something." Taylor almost whispered the words.

"What's up?"

I heard the fear in her voice. "I'm pregnant."

Excitement and concern arose in me. *Wow, she's going to be a mom! Oh, my gosh — she's going to be a mom! Who's the father?*

"Congratulations. I love you, Taylor."

What more could I say? I thought I understood where God wanted me after that.

I decided to move back to Gig Harbor to be with my sister and help her however I could.

☙☙☙

The University of Idaho campus ministry gifted me with an incredible six years. They showed me what it looked like to love others and put them before myself. Moving back to Gig Harbor meant that it was time for me to go out and serve a new community.

On a visit home in my last year of graduate school, I had decided to check out one of the local churches, Harbor Life.

Pastor Tyson greeted me like an old friend as soon as I walked in.

I had a flashback to move-in day my freshman year when Luke helped us out.

As I finished up graduate school, I prayed for God to show me where I could best serve. I couldn't get the image and feel of Harbor Life out of my head.

Late one night I sent an email:

Pastor Tyson,

God is telling me to be a part of your church community. If you need me to scrub toilets, I will scrub toilets. I love scrubbing toilets. Please let me know how I can help you.

Pastor Tyson responded:

Kyle,

I am very excited to have you be a part of our community! Please tell me more about yourself. I like to think our toilets stay pretty clean, but I believe you can help in other areas. I can't wait to get to know you better!

Pastor Tyson and Harbor Life Church have been an important part of my life ever since. They have unflinchingly supported, encouraged and grown with me for the past five years.

My wife, Brianna, and I got married after I had been in the church for about a year and a half. Pastor Tyson officiated at our ceremony, and many members of Harbor Life and my group of friends from college ministry attended, showing love and support.

తతతత

Most youth ministers will say it takes years of ministry before you have a student express your impact on him or her. I am no exception.

RECALIBRATE

After five years of involvement with the youth at Harbor Life Church, one of the teens, Phillip, shared one of these moments with me. His attendance record was spotty at best, but when he did show up, I always cherished our talks. I tried to show him he mattered to me — love him however I could. His senior year of high school, he asked me to write him a letter of recommendation, and I happily obliged.

Three months ago, I received a letter from him:

> Kyle,
>
> I just wanted to say thank you. I know I did not always show up to youth group, but you never held it against me. I've never had someone care for me like you did. You listened to all of the problems with my family and always knew what to say. Thank you for the letter you wrote, but most of all, thank you for being there for me.
> Sincerely,
> Phillip

It still blows my mind that God loves the deepest, darkest parts of me more than anyone could love even my best façade. *That's* the kind of love I need and strive to show others in my life today.

NEVER ALONE
The Story of Elizabeth
Written by Ameerah Collins

"Don't blame yourself, Elizabeth." Dr. Maxwell tilted his head and regarded me with squinted eyes. "What you're feeling is perfectly normal. Now that your sons are going off to college and starting their own lives, your reality has become …" he paused, looking for the right words, "more visible than before."

"Ugh." I slumped over in the plush chair and rubbed my forehead. "How could I have been so blind? I let the love for and from my children mask my marital issues."

"Hey." Dr. Maxwell tossed his pad on the mahogany desk beside us and leaned toward me. "I can see you're hurting, Elizabeth. As we've discussed before, it's time for the pain to end. In cases like yours, a divorce is acceptable. Infidelity, verbal abuse, refusal to receive marriage counseling for possible reconciliation — this all constitutes a breaking of the marriage vows."

"I understand all that." I shook my head and peered up at Dr. Maxwell. "But when is a good time to tell my husband we need to separate? How do I tell him I no longer want to be part of this marriage? That it's so draining and depressing. When should I do all that? My son is graduating soon. I can't just spring this on my family so suddenly."

Dr. Maxwell leaned back in his chair. "Elizabeth, there

is never a good time to break up a marriage. Something will always come up, and you'll always use it as a reason or excuse to hold off the separation."

I groaned. "He's a wonderful father. He's just a horrible husband. It'll hurt him."

Demand a divorce. End my marriage. Split up my family. Become single again.

"I'm not sure if I can do this to him, to my sons, to us."

"Sometimes you have to do what's best for *you*, Elizabeth."

ৡৡৡ

I didn't experience a troubled childhood or any significant events that would have an adverse effect on me in adulthood. I lived a fairly normal life as a kid with my big brother, two younger brothers, Mom and my stepfather. During my teenage years, I began hanging around with the wrong crowd. The sort of youngsters who skipped school and attended the usual high school parties every now and then. I never did anything wild or crazy, I was just the typical kid. Your standard teenybopper.

It wasn't until after graduation that my life completely changed. I married my boyfriend, Marlon. He had a few years on me and had already endured a rough divorce, but he had full custody of his son, Landon. Knowing the court awarded Marlon with full custody increased my confidence in him as a good man. Without question, I took Landon in as my own son and raised him from when

he was just a baby boy. I never deemed him my stepson —
I thought of him as my own.

For a while, I believed I had the perfect marriage.
Marlon and I did everything together. He willingly
accompanied me on my shopping trips and even tagged
along when my mother and I went grocery shopping. As
we pushed the cart together, playing with Landon in the
child seat, Marlon usually stayed a few steps behind.

"You don't think that's a little odd?" Mom whispered
as she chucked a head of lettuce in the cart. She jerked her
head toward Marlon. "You know. Marlon. The fact that he
feels the need to go everywhere you go? That's not weird
to you?"

"I don't know." I glanced over my shoulder and smiled
at Marlon. I shrugged. "I guess he just likes to be around
me. Or maybe he's protective over Landon and me."

"It's a bit bodyguard-like, don't you think?"

I chuckled as Mom cut her eyes at Marlon once more.
"Relax, Mom. It's not a big deal."

"Hmm." She pursed her lips, then softly smiled.
"Okay, sweetheart. Whatever you say."

❧❧❧

Years later, I realized Mom's early suspicions were
right on. As Landon grew older, and after I gave birth to
Jasper and then Stephen, what seemed at first like
protectiveness became overbearing and uncomfortable. I
hadn't truly noticed Marlon's constant fascination with

my whereabouts or continuous need to hover around me until my three boys grew older and no longer needed me to baby them.

Whenever I left the house, he questioned when I'd return or insisted on running my errands with me. Marlon had grown so accustomed to me being a "stay-at-home mom" to our children that when they reached high school and I began working as a store manager, he became paranoid and questioned my loyalty to him.

"Where the hell have you been, Elizabeth?" Marlon rounded on me as soon as I stepped into our house. I sighed as he trailed behind me into the living room, and I flopped onto the sofa.

"Please don't yell," I mumbled and rubbed my eyes. "I've had a long night."

"Forget that!" he huffed, and the stench of rank alcohol flowed from his mouth. "You're 20 minutes late! You're cheating on me, aren't you?"

"Oh, my gosh," I groaned. I rested my head against the back of the sofa and shut my eyes. "For once, can I just get through the door before you start in on your crazy accusations?"

"Where were you, huh? You stop at some poor bastard's house? Did you?"

I opened my eyes to see Marlon looming over me with his hands clenched at his side.

"Would you just take a chill pill for one moment? I'm not cheating on you. I just had to stay over for a bit. There was some paperwork I had to —"

"Shut up, Elizabeth." Marlon began pacing the carpet. "I don't want to hear your lies. I'm not dumb. Ever since you lost a few pounds, you've gotten beside yourself. You get a little attention from a few guys, and you think you can do better than me. Is that it?"

I hopped up from the couch, and he halted in front of me. "Lost a few pounds? Really, Marlon? For one, it was 55 pounds. And the only reason," I pointed a finger in his face, "I lost that much weight was because of your endless nagging, your controlling ways and your lack of trust in me. *You* exhaust *me*, Marlon. I have been so depressed dealing with your crap. You don't even know!"

"Whatever." Marlon stomped down the hall, and I fell back against the couch.

"Whatever yourself," I barely whispered.

Over the next few months, Marlon continued to question me about my supposed unfaithfulness to him. Every evening I stepped in the door from work, he gave me the third degree.

He even showed up at my job just to reprimand me for spending too much time with the vendors or male workers. He saw me as a big cheat, and nothing I said convinced him otherwise.

For a while, I blamed the accusations on his possible insecurities or need for control, but when I found out Marlon actually cheated on *me* twice, I realized the source of his paranoia. He probably figured since he'd cheated, I'd do the same. I wasn't anything like Marlon, though. I believe he knew that deep down.

RECALIBRATE

One day my mother visited me at work and gasped at my appearance.

"Honey." Mom cupped my cheek with her warm hand. "Your skin is so pale. You've lost even more weight, and not the healthy sort. You look terrible, Elizabeth. What's going on?"

I whimpered and eased around Mom to close my office door. My mother engulfed me in her arms and rubbed my back. I couldn't do anything but stand there and revert into a helpless little girl.

"Is it Marlon, sweetheart?" Mom's soft voice vibrated against my scalp, and I nodded my head. "He hasn't hurt you, has he? He didn't put his hands on you, did he?"

"N-n-no, Mom. Of course not." I eased out of her arms and sat on the edge of my desk. "Nothing like that. He's just not the *Marlon* I married, or at least, I don't think so. He's always drunk. And maybe it's the liquor talking, but he makes these ridiculous claims against me all the time. He's so adamant that I'm having an affair. He insists that there are so many obvious signs of me cheating. I can't even come home late from work or make a few friends without him going berserk. He even comes to my job to keep tabs on me, Mom. He's disrupting my work!"

I resisted the urge to scream.

"I'm just so sick of Marlon and his crap."

Mom shushed me and massaged my shoulders. "It'll be okay, Elizabeth. You'll get through this. I always knew I saw something off about Marlon's behavior with you, but I didn't think it'd get this out of hand. Usually when men act this way it's due to their own insecurities, an actual paranoia disorder — or infidelity. I'm so sorry, honey."

"Yeah," I hiccuped, wiping my tears. "Tell me about it. He's cheated, Mom. *Twice.* He's been an overprotective guy all our married life, but now he's just this insensitive, domineering jerk. I hate it. I don't know how much more of this I can take. I feel so alone, which is nuts because *he's always there* — watching me like a hawk. I'm so angry. I'm either angry or sad, never happy."

"You can't let him do that, Elizabeth. Don't let this change you."

"I can't help it," I said, sighing. "I think we need to see someone or something."

"I agree. Seek marriage counseling. If that doesn't work, then at least you tried."

ॐॐॐ

Later, I approached Marlon about seeing a marriage counselor. He refused to involve a third party in our problems, so I planned on going alone.

"Oh, no." Marlon laughed without an ounce of humor. "You're not going by yourself, Elizabeth. You're probably going to meet some guy. Like I said before, I know you're having an affair. This marriage counseling crap is an act. No way am I letting you go alone."

"Meet some guy? Affair?" I rolled my eyes and stalked toward the kitchen with Marlon on my heels. "Would you listen to yourself? I'm not seeing anyone else but you. I'm trying to save our marriage. A marriage you obviously no longer care about."

"Like I said —" Marlon raided the refrigerator while I started in on the dishes. "You're not going alone. I'll drop you off and wait for you in the parking lot."

"And that right there," I pointed at him with soapsuds covering my hands, "is precisely why I'm going in the first place. You're paranoid for no good reason."

"Whatever," he mumbled. "I gotta keep an eye on you."

The day I went to visit Dr. Maxwell, Marlon did exactly what he said he'd do. He drove me to the office, then waited in the parking lot for my session to end. I sat in a chair with Dr. Maxwell seated next to me and his large desk just inches away. Surprisingly, we didn't talk much about my marriage or Marlon. He seemed to focus on everything in my life besides Marlon, which wasn't much.

"You mention your sons quite a bit during our conversation." Dr. Maxwell sat crossed-legged with his foot tapping his knee and his notepad resting on his lap. "You obviously adore your sons, but can you tell me more about your relationship with them?"

"My sons." I grinned as their faces popped in my mind. "Well, as you know, my oldest is actually my stepson. No one would ever know it, though. I consider Landon my first little one. I'm the only mother he's ever known, and whatever happens between his father and me, I'll always be his mother. He *is* my son. I love him as if my own blood runs through him."

"Wow." Dr. Maxwell jotted a few notes on his pad. "You have a lot of love, Elizabeth."

I chuckled. "I suppose that's where my middle son, Jasper, gets it from. He's always been lovable. As a child, he'd randomly tell me, 'Mom, you're so beautiful,' or he'd hug me and say, 'I love you, Mom.' He's special, Jasper."

"And your other one? You mentioned a third son before, correct?"

"Right," I said, nodding. "Stephen is my youngest. He's 15 years old. I feel like just yesterday I was changing his diaper and waking up in the middle of the night to fix him a bottle. He's now in high school. Jasper is graduating soon. And Landon has grown up so fast. Sometimes I wonder where the time has gone. You know?"

"They're leaving the nest soon, huh?" Dr. Maxwell smiled softly.

"Yeah." I shrugged. "They've always been there. Even when things between Marlon and I were less than perfect, my children have always been the constant love and joy in my life."

"I want to stop for a minute, Elizabeth." Dr. Maxwell tossed his notepad on his desk and uncrossed his legs. He gazed at me for a few seconds, then tilted his head. "It's almost as if your sons *are* your life and have been for a while now. Earlier and just now, you didn't truly touch on your husband as much as a wife usually would. Why is that?"

I laughed sharply. "Well, besides the negative, there isn't much to say. Our problems stretch far and wide, and he's not even here with me. He's in the parking lot —" I threw my hands up, "being the ever-controlling and untrusting man he is. I wanted him to come with me, but he's just — Marlon and I just aren't the same. We're not who we used to be."

"Hmm." He clasped his hands. "I don't believe you're in love with your husband anymore. Honestly, I believe you fell out of love with him many years ago. Your children have filled that void in which you desired love. They gave you the love your marriage lacked."

Puzzled, I asked, "What do you mean? I'm not sure I understand."

"Well, when you first fell in love with Marlon, you also fell in love with Landon — a precious gift you could love on and call your own. Then you had Jasper. He said adorable things Marlon should have told you. And Stephen, another gift to mask the reality of your marriage."

"Oh, my goodness!" I gasped at Dr. Maxwell's deduction. "That makes so much sense. How could I have been so blind? How could I miss that?"

After that first session, I met with Dr. Maxwell several more times over the course of two months to discuss my marriage. Unfortunately, Marlon never came to marriage counseling with me. He continued to spew accusations at me, hurt me with his words and disregard my efforts to resolve our issues. He just couldn't get over his controlling ways, and I didn't want to keep being subjected to them anymore.

Before long, Dr. Maxwell suggested that it might be time to separate from Marlon. I didn't realize that getting a divorce would hurt us so badly, but it did. I knew he had control and trust issues, and our marriage was crumbling before our eyes, but I still thought Marlon was an awesome father. At one point in our lives, I truly believe we loved one another. We raised three sons together. Marlon and I had our dilemmas, but part of me still cared for him when I requested that divorce. Part of me felt guilty when I watched him ask for another chance. But, I knew we didn't belong together.

So, I ended it.

જ્જ્જ

A month after our separation, my son Stephen and I moved into a new apartment. Jasper and Landon both prepared to join the military. Living the single life in my late "flirty 30s" seemed to get to me.

Ironically, I began to act in ways that would have warranted Marlon's suspicions. I convinced myself that I needed to get out, meet guys, have a fun time and simply live out my newfound freedom. However, I also harbored deep hatred in my heart toward all men. I wanted them to hurt just as I had been hurt in my marriage.

Oftentimes, I studied my reflection in the mirror. I knew I could capture the attention of any man I desired, so I set out to be a heartbreaker. Hanging out at the bar all night, I saw how quickly the fellas flocked toward me, and getting them to cater to me came so easily.

RECALIBRATE

During the day, I was the sweetest girl in the world. I treated people nicely and equally, I continued to show my sons the utmost love and care and I kept a smile on my face. However, at night, I became this fun-loving seductress with three simple goals in mind: pick up a guy, make him fall for me, then dump him. It gave me control and power — the sort of control and power I had lacked in my marriage. And I loved it.

"I'm just looking to have fun," I always told the men. "I don't want a relationship, so don't go falling for me. I can guarantee you, I won't fall back."

I informed guys upfront about my intentions, so I wouldn't feel guilty if they actually started to care for me. It was my way of protecting myself. Although I voiced the warning to them, I still did everything in my power to make them love me. I also behaved in a manner that made them believe I loved them — eyeing them with sultry looks, bringing them back to my place and making them feel at home, and acting jealous when I knew I really didn't care what they did or who they entertained outside of my presence.

When men made the mistake of saying, "I think I love you, Elizabeth," I'd always reply, "I don't know where that sudden devotion of love came from, but you better put it back in your mouth. I don't want anything to do with it. I told you I wasn't looking for love. You knew that."

"Geez, Elizabeth. Way to break a guy's heart," they usually said.

"Can't say I didn't warn you."

I did this repeatedly and never felt bad about it. For more than three years, I had a married man wrapped so tightly around my finger that he hated the thought of knowing I fooled around with others guys and not only him. Ronnie wanted so badly to be in control of me, but I wouldn't allow it.

When he stayed home with his wife, I made sure he knew I already had a date for the evening. Sometimes he even left home and drove around town searching for me to have me to himself. When he traveled for business trips, I always had another guy vying for my attention.

"Elizabeth!" Ronnie barked over the phone one night. "Where are you? I've been driving all over town, checking out the bars and all. I can't find you."

"Shouldn't you be home with your wife, Ronnie?" I nestled my cell phone against my ear, stirred my drink and smirked at the ladies sitting at the bar with me. "You know, that's not very husbandly of you to leave her like that. Believe me, I know."

"Cut the crap, Elizabeth. Just tell me where you are. I'm coming to you."

"Oh, calm down. I'm just out with my girls. I haven't caught anyone for the night, just yet." I covered the receiver and giggled softly.

"That's not funny."

"Oh, buck up, Ronnie." I chuckled when he sighed. "You need not worry about me. Go back home to your little wife, and I'll see you another night. After all, I'm just your little side piece. You'd do good to remember that."

I hung up, but just moments later he burst through the bar entrance and strutted toward me. I swiveled around in my stool and eyed him.

"I found you." He sat beside me.

"It never fails." I laughed. "You always do."

After playing these games for three and a half years, I grew tired of the absence of real love and friendship in my life. The ladies I hung out with at the bars were simply my drinking buddies, nothing more. I didn't confide in them about my anger toward men and warped desire to hurt nearly every man I came across. They didn't know much about my past marriage. They just thought of me as a fun gal.

I wanted to experience a relationship in which a man actually loved me for me and not my seductive, flirtatious act. I wanted to be able to call someone and simply say, "Hi," instead of my usual, "You want to come over for a while?" Nothing in my lifestyle at that time allowed room for me to have the true friends I wanted versus the party friends I had.

So, I decided to give it all up. I stripped away my heartbreaker status, cut out the late-night drinking — and drunk driving — and stopped bringing men home.

I started seeing a therapist.

"You're depressed," my therapist told me. "And you're lonely. You're very alone."

Well, go figure.

Although my therapist prescribed me pills for my depression, I couldn't shake the loneliness I felt deep within. I eventually created an online profile for a dating site, but when a man messaged me, I got chicken feet and pushed him away. I told him I had a busy work schedule at that time, and I wouldn't have much time to chat with him. That didn't stop him, though. Just two weeks later, he messaged me again.

Oh, man, I thought. *How am I going to get out of this? I should have never responded. But maybe I'll give him a chance. After all the crap I've done to guys, I should give him a shot.*

I went out with Jeremy and noticed how different he seemed from every other man I'd ever encountered. He didn't drink or appear to have a mean streak. He didn't merely want me as some kind of chick on the side. He wished for a serious relationship. And what really stuck out to me was that Jeremy refused to fall for my flirty looks or sweet talk. He didn't want me to put on a show.

He just wanted *me*.

❧❧❧

Jeremy and I dated for nearly four years before we got married. During that time, I learned Jeremy had gone to college to become a youth pastor, and for years, he'd lived a life dedicated to the Lord.

I didn't really understand everything he said about his time in church or even care to fully comprehend it all. I'd never considered myself a God-fearing person. I actually didn't even believe in God. I'd heard about Jesus and God as a little girl, but I didn't think much about them.

Not until I met Jeremy, anyway.

"I don't feel right anymore, Elizabeth." Jeremy sat beside me at our kitchen table and sipped at his drink. "I need to get back in church. I'm not where God wants me to be. I know it."

"Okay." I shrugged, not really understanding why it was bothering him so badly. "I know you've said that plenty of times before, but why don't we just find a church and start going?"

"It's not that simple. I'm missing the connection I once had with him. I'm a backslider, Elizabeth. Do you know what that is?"

"No." I shifted in my chair uncomfortably. "What is it?"

"It's when you've turned your back on God and he's no longer the center of your life. It's similar to rebelling against your father, someone who once held your heart in his hands, and needing to ask that father for forgiveness. I haven't stopped trusting in God. I still believe Jesus died for my wrongdoing, but I've closed my heart to him. I walked away from God, Elizabeth. He never walked away from me. And that's eating me up inside."

"I'm surprised you walked away. It seems like you really loved him."

"I did. *I do.*" Jeremy sighed. "It's just not the same. I need to find a church. Soon."

I didn't totally understand Jeremy's sadness regarding his departure from God, but I knew I wanted to make him happy. Although I hoped for Jeremy to find his peace again, I believed joining a church would simply be a nice hobby for us — allowing us to spend quality time together.

When we visited Harbor Life Church, I enjoyed the joyous singing, friendly faces and inspirational speaking. I liked sitting next to my husband and basking in something he cherished so deeply and genuinely seemed to be emotionally touched by. The church members knew Jeremy had a special relationship with God, mainly more so than I, and that I didn't really do the whole Christian thing, but they welcomed me, anyway.

The love they showed me intrigued me.

"Hey, Elizabeth!" Paula, a church member I'd become friends with, caught up with me after gathering one afternoon. "You should think about joining the Alpha program we're starting."

"The Alpha program? What's that?"

"Well," Paula said, beaming, "it's a 10-week course for new Christians or people who simply want to know more about the Bible. It's a way to introduce someone to Jesus."

I wrung my hands.

"Hmm, I'm not sure about that, Paula. Let me think about it."

I was uncertain about joining the Alpha program because I never expected to become involved with any church activities or functions. I just wanted to spend time with my husband and enjoy seeing him finding the peace he felt he'd lost. After various folks started telling me more about the Alpha program and suggesting I join it, I finally agreed.

During the course, we watched videos of a man who'd once been far from Jesus talk about how he came to know him in a personal way. The videos intrigued me.

The spokesman talked about developing a personal relationship with Christ and allowing him to enter your heart. The videos also explained various books of the Bible, and surprisingly, I understood every word.

After each video, the class split into groups to discuss the content of the day's clip. While everyone else seemed to have some sort of knowledge regarding God, I was lacking in that area. However, teachers and fellow members of the Alpha program all gathered around me, answered the questions that puzzled me and never looked down on me for not knowing as much as they did. Their acceptance and friendliness brought me closer to God. They helped open my mind to believe that one day I could possibly open my heart to Jesus. And that he'd actually come in.

I found myself wanting the joy they had. I wanted to experience the easy happiness they found in Christ Jesus. Even though I knew they most likely had their fair share of pain and troubling times, they still found tranquility in God. I saw God in them. *How could they do that?*

The class prompted me to conduct my own outside research. Each day, I set aside time to study the Bible and try to truly get to know Jesus. I didn't understand every word I read, and Jeremy suggested I buy a children's Bible for easier reading, but honestly, that kind of insulted me. I didn't want to read the children's Bible — I wanted to read the Bible my classmates read. Whenever I didn't grasp a concept, I rushed to Jeremy or Paula to help me figure it out.

Another activity that didn't come so easy to me was prayer. I talked to God in my mind while driving through town, cleaning the house or cooking dinner, but I didn't know how to speak my prayers out loud, especially in the company of others. When Jeremy and I prayed together, I usually let him do the talking. By then, I knew he'd grown closer to God and opened himself back up to Jesus, so I felt better with him leading our prayer.

"Elizabeth." Jeremy nudged my shoulder one evening as we knelt at our bedside in prayer. I peeked at him from behind my clasped hands and smiled. "If you have something you need to say, or you have a prayer you want to get off your chest, just step in and do so."

"Um." I bit my lip. "Okay, I'll step in when I feel comfortable."

Jeremy chuckled. "Good."

Eventually, I began saying more during my prayer time with my husband.

"Lord," I said one night, "please protect my sons and grandchildren. I, uh, I know they're on their own life journeys, but I ask that you step into their lives and show yourself to them just as you did me. I was once an atheist. I doubted your existence so heavily, God, but I don't anymore." I stopped and cleared my throat as my eyes watered. "Please touch Landon's mind and heart. I want him to give you a chance. Please protect Jasper. I know he's going through so much right now, and he may not know it, but he needs you so badly. And I pray that Stephen one day believes in you, God. He's so smart, and he's such an intellectual. I know he's a hard nut to crack, but I know you can break his walls down, Jesus. I know you can."

I looked over at Jeremy with his hands clasped against his forehead. I nudged him, he glanced at me and I quietly said, "I'm done." Instantly, he took over. After that first night, I started speaking my prayers out to God more frequently. I even started leading the prayers, with Jeremy adding here and there.

Steadily, I grew bolder with my faith in God, and I knew I needed to officially give my life to Christ. However, as I studied the Bible, I read passages that addressed God's stance on divorce. I saw where he disapproved of it. The way I understood it, God wanted us to stay with our spouses and stick it out. So I needed to ask Pastor Tyson if God would forgive me for my divorce. I believed God would forgive me for hurting all the men from my past and taking my pain out on them, I just wasn't sure about the divorce part.

"I'm thinking about accepting the Lord," I told him. Jeremy and I sat across from Pastor Tyson in his office, with our hands laced. "I just have some questions first."

"By all means." Pastor Tyson nodded with an easy smile. "Shoot."

"Okay. So, I know what the Bible states about divorce. And the fact that both Jeremy and I have been divorced concerns me. Will God forgive me for my separation from my first husband? Or is it simply unforgivable? I need some reassurance that I'm not a horrible person. You know? Is there a point in which God won't accept someone?"

"I understand your concerns, Elizabeth. However, we must remember that God is a forgiving God. As long as you possess a sincere heart to ask God for forgiveness, and you truly feel sorry for your past wrongdoing, God won't pass you over. You can be forgiven."

I nodded. "Okay. That's reassuring."

"If you don't mind, can you tell me why you sought a divorce for your first marriage?"

"Our marriage wasn't based on, um, I guess you could say Biblical principles. I didn't believe in God then, and neither did Marlon. My husband was very controlling. He constantly accused me of having an affair, when it was actually he who cheated on me. I didn't like the way he talked to me — sometimes it was quite mean and insulting. I tried marriage counseling to possibly reconcile us, but he refused to try that. Marlon has always been an awesome father but not a great husband for me."

"Here's the deal, Elizabeth," Pastor Tyson said. "One of the greatest aspects of accepting Jesus into your heart and connecting with him on a personal level is the knowledge he gives you about himself. I know God is a loving God, just as you do. Therefore, I believe God makes exceptions for situations such as your past marriage. He doesn't want any of his children to hurt. The person you marry shouldn't be the one who hurts you the most. God doesn't like that. You said you didn't believe then, correct?"

I nodded. "Right."

"When we don't have Christ in our lives, sometimes we make bad decisions that were never aligned with God's path for us. Once we go to God, he forgives us for making those decisions, too."

"Wow. I never saw it like that."

"Hmmm." Pastor Tyson grinned. "Isn't God amazing? A marriage shouldn't be built upon lies, mistrust and betrayal. It should be built on Jesus Christ and his principles. Because when everything in your marriage is falling apart, you and your spouse can equally come to Jesus and ask him for help. That's what you and Jeremy can have."

"If God can forgive me for everything in my past, then I want to be part of his life, and I want him to be part of mine."

Pastor Tyson prayed with Jeremy and me. I accepted the Lord into my life and claimed him as my one and only God. I asked him for forgiveness and proclaimed my belief in his son, Jesus Christ.

At the next church gathering, I announced my newfound commitment to the Lord, and everyone cheered and congratulated me.

I felt so loved, revived and free.

ॐॐॐ

NEVER ALONE

Ever since I gave my life to God, I found myself wanting everyone to know about him and his greatness. I made sure to study my Bible, pray to God and continuously focus my thoughts on him. At first, I didn't really see a difference in myself, but everyone else did.

"Elizabeth!" My friends cornered me at church. "There's a huge difference in you. You're like a light. You're so bright. My goodness, you're glowing!"

Just knowing other folks saw me growing in Jesus pushed me to continue my journey to get as close to him as possible. Their words also placed me on a mission to tell my family and friends about God and what he'd done for me. He saved me from the feelings of loneliness I'd dealt with for so long. He rescued me from living a life without him — and what an unfulfilling life that would have been! Jesus altered my heart and gave me more empathy and love for others, especially those in need.

He warmed me. Inside and out.

God even allowed me to be a voice to my son Jasper. For so long, he'd been going through a rough time in his life, and he really needed guidance that nobody seemed able to offer him. I practically begged him to give God a try. I asked him to let Jesus in until he finally did.

"I did what you told me to do, Mom," Jasper said over the phone. His voice sounded a bit shaken, like he'd witnessed something surreal. "I asked God to help me, and the most incredible thing happened. Something kept pushing me to skim through those papers I told you about, and I tried to push the thought out. But it kept banging at my head, telling me to look. And when I finally did, I saw something in the papers I'd never seen before."

"Wow," I said. "You see what prayer can do?"

"If I hadn't looked over those papers again, I would have gotten myself in a horrible situation. I think God saved me from that trouble, Mom. I believe he helped me."

Not long after God revealed himself to Jasper in a personal way, my son gave his life to the Lord. For a few years, I'd prayed that God would lend a hand to Jasper and let him know how real and awesome he is. I saw that God didn't cast my prayer aside; instead, I believe he honored it and answered it.

Just like God enabled me to talk to my son and touch Jasper's heart, I'm praying that he does the same for Landon and Stephen. And not just my sons, but all my family members, friends and even people who are strangers to me.

I want everyone to experience the greatness of God on earth. I want them to spread the love of Jesus and introduce others to Christ. I want to see them all in heaven someday. Although I want to see Jesus in heaven, I'd love to bring family, friends and random strangers with me.

I believe God protected me when I didn't even know him. I saw how God loved me despite my refusal to love him or even believe in him, for that matter. My wish is for people to know there is a loving and gracious God who can take their pain away. To know there is a God who will dry your tears and replace your weeping heart with one full of joy.

That doesn't mean life will be perfect — I still cry sometimes, feeling bad for the guys I recklessly hurt.

It doesn't mean days will always be super easy — I still ache knowing not all my sons have Jesus.

It doesn't mean an end to suffering — I still have my struggles, my aches and pains.

However, everything got so much easier with God on my side. Life was so doable when I learned to hand my problems over to the Lord. Living wasn't so hard with Jesus guiding my footsteps.

As long as we have God, we'll never be alone. Even when we don't realize he's there.

He is.

A CRY FOR PEACE
The Story of
Ezekiel and Laura
Written by Amy Jones

I grabbed my friend Mustaffah and fled the bank where we worked. Our hearts raced as we ran to my car. The riots and violence were escalating all around the city. That morning's religious protests heated up enough to send us home for the day. We had to get to Mustaffah's mom.

We feared she might already be dead. As the owner of a hotel with a restaurant and bar, her business risked being targeted in the unrest.

Mustaffah spotted her along the curb — safe and unharmed. I slowed, and he pulled her into the car. We looked around and saw angry mobs of violent radicals slaughtering innocent people in the very street where we drove, police attempting to rescue the living and flames burning mosques and churches.

Police blockades kept us in downtown Kaduna for quite some time. Once allowed to pass, we quickly headed for the back roads, hoping for a safe journey home. We nearly made it to the outskirts of the uprising when a group of five men stopped us. Farther down the road waited other groups of five to 10 men as far as I could see. I kept repeating two thoughts in my head:

How do I get Mustaffah and his mom home safely?

RECALIBRATE

How do I get home?

Mobs like these killed without discrimination, making our desperate situation potentially deadly. My brain told my foot to hit the brakes. Bodies lay dead in the streets. Machine guns, menacing men and machetes blurred in and out of my vision. Thick black smoke billowed high in the air above heaping piles of burning tires.

Impulses of fear sent my mind racing and my heart pounding.

The horrific images became snapshots of genocide, mental pictures I would not soon forget.

Mustaffah's mother pointed out what looked like a disorderly lot of abandoned vehicles. And the smell — oh, the smell! A nauseating, eerie mix of death, hate, intent and burning rubber permeated my vehicle. The air smelled poisonous with this thick, sticky, messy smell. Mustaffah bravely voiced what all three of us were thinking, "Those dead bodies were once tucked safely in those abandoned cars. How long do you suppose we will stay alive in this BMW?"

The pounding thud of rocks began to pelt my little car from all over. The men approached our vehicle with eyes full of hate — and a seemingly infinite supply of rocks and artillery.

ॐॐॐ

Nigeria has roughly half the population of the United States, yet squeezes them into a geographical area not quite twice the size of California. The population is almost exactly split between Christians and Muslims. The Muslims reside primarily in the North, and Christians in the South.

I'd lived in Nigeria all my life and already witnessed political crises and religious uprisings before the Zangon-Kataf riots of 1992. I'd already been through the Zaria crisis of 1980 and two other major events of civil unrest in 1982 and 1987.

Nigeria is in West Africa, and its roots run deep with cultural battles between various people groups. There are many excuses given why these outbursts happen, but each boils down to a fundamental difference in religious motive. The Muslims desire to institute Sharī'ah law into the governing forces. As a result, they treat Christians as "infidels" who need to be eliminated by the Muslims. Heavy persecution and frustration among the Christian population is the result. Sharī'ah law is an Islamic law, and it is the only way, or path, according to Muslims. The law's desire is to govern and regulate people in all aspects of their lives according to a legal system taken from the Islamic book of the Qur'an. Sharī'ah law manifests itself by telling people how to dress, what to eat and where to worship when under its oppressive hand. Unfortunately, it also means putting to death anyone who does not want to follow its rules.

The eldest of four children, I was raised in a Christian home. My parents moved to the capital city of Kaduna before any of us were born. Kaduna State is in the North-

RECALIBRATE

West zone of Nigeria, Muslim country. Kaduna State is the hotspot for religious crisis in Nigeria. Every argument originates from complex ethnic, religious and regional divisions. Despite these frictions in the larger community, my family lived in an integrated neighborhood of Muslims and Christians.

Growing up, I knew little of the fierce divisions. I just knew I wanted to hang out with my friends, both Muslim and Christian. I valued their friendships, and over time we grew close. I loved them all like brothers.

But propaganda and pressure from religious leaders got the best of my friends' parents. The winds of hatred came and blew the last remnant of our deep, trusting friendships down the dusty roads of Kaduna. My heart broke as family after family turned on each other with spite and suspicion. It happened so fast I still wore perfume from my Muslim friend Abdal's mother on the front of my shirts.

I often thought back with fondness for Abdal's mom. Mrs. Ibrahim was a special lady and a wonderful cook. Over a period of weeks and months, our neighborhood became torn in every direction. Occasionally, I would pull out another pungent cotton shirt doused with the musky smell favored by Mrs. Ibrahim. It made me long for simpler times. I realized some shirts were better left dodging the laundry a little while longer.

I served God alongside my parents throughout my childhood and teenage years. They taught me scripture, took me to a loving church and, by example, led me in how to follow Christ. I cannot remember a time when I didn't consider myself a Christian. My parents knew how to pray. They prayed for their children, one another and the people God placed in their lives. I learned young how important it was for the church to stick together. It was the only way we were going to survive the hell of persecution.

When riots started to break out in the streets of Kaduna, random people would be stopped and asked, "What is your name?" If your name gave you away as a Christian, you might be shot and killed.

If a person managed to live through the first question, they'd be probed with another, "Are you Christian or Muslim?" Many Christians replied "Muslim" to save their lives.

Unfortunately, they were not prepared for the last and final demand, "Quote me something out of the Qur'an." At this point, at a loss for words, many Christians' earthly lives came to an end.

The ethnic establishment of Nigeria came about in the 1800s, and with it came Muslim and Christian conflict. Christians remained tolerant of their persecution for nearly 200 years, but by the time the 1992 Zangon-Kataf riots hit, they had had enough. Out of desperation, they decided to retaliate. Some Westerners may dispute this decision. They point out Jesus' teachings of "loving your enemies and praying for those who persecute you." I agree with that stance, but I can also identify with my Nigerian brothers and sisters who have watched the people dearest to them be tortured generation after generation. Suffice it to say, the Christian retaliation of 1992 sent a clear message of frustration to their Muslim counterparts.

Soon, more mobs of people appeared throughout the city — residents of Kaduna who encountered mobs had to ask themselves, *Are we Muslim or Christian?* The answer to that question could mean life or death.

Radical Christian groups started stopping Muslims. They would ask their name, religious affiliation and for a Bible quote. The tables turned. Some say it was survival — others, self-defense.

Whatever the reason, it was a guaranteed recipe for a no-win situation.

❧❧❧

I was working for a bank in 1994. Ninety percent of employees in my corporation were Muslim.

Our professional lives were quite peaceful as long as the country remained calm, but the moment things started to heat up, Christian employees were targeted as untrustworthy and looked at with suspicion by Islamic co-workers.

One day, my Muslim boss abruptly approached me about the religious uprising that had broken out hours before. "There are riots in the streets, Ezekiel. The fighting has gotten very bad. You have a choice: You may leave work now or stay and take your chances."

"I would like to leave now, if it's okay," I muttered

with a voice as stone cold as my demeanor. Something told me this crisis was going to be different. I knew I needed to get home before the Muslims blocked the road to my neighborhood. Before we left, a handful of us met together in a conference room to pray for peace in our country and for the safety of our Christian brothers and sisters. Afterward, I grabbed Mustaffah and left. I was fortunate enough to own my BMW, but Mustaffah didn't have that luxury. Neither did his mom. I needed to help them get home safely because violence could escalate fast.

With riots worsening, a government shutdown looked imminent. If that was the case, the bank wouldn't reopen for a week. In shutdowns, we were ordered to stay put. If you were like Mustaffah and his mother, this meant you would live in your place of employment until the sanctions let up simply because you had no transportation home. I'm not sure he was thankful for the ride once we started home and faced the sight of freshly murdered bodies and the smell of burning tires.

As the thud of rocks pelted the BMW, none of us thought we would escape. But thanks to the grace of God over us, and the prayers of my co-workers in the conference room, all three of us did eventually safely reach our homes.

ॐॐॐ

During the next week, tensions grew. I kept abreast of events by watching the news and talking with other

Christians. Muslims began to burn the churches and homes of Christians. Then Christians torched mosques and destroyed Islamic homes. Neighbor turned against neighbor. Christians who lived in Muslim neighborhoods were forbidden to enter their homes. Consequently, they were taken in to live with other Christians.

We lived in a neighborhood peppered with several different types of homes, including apartments and single-family dwellings. Just down the paved streets were several schools, mosques, churches and businesses.

We were ordered by the government to take cover daily from 6 p.m. to 6 a.m. I felt like my family and I were prisoners in our home. During those long night hours, the men took watch over our homes and neighborhoods, using guns and machetes to protect against Muslim threat and attack. My father and I witnessed Muslims slipping through the bushes in our neighborhood, attacking our neighbors and burning down their homes. Our Christian neighbors escaped. Once their houses were destroyed, they sought refuge in the homes of their Christian friends.

Fortunately, we were not attacked. It is a good thing, too, because we did not choose to fight with guns and knives. We relied on God to supernaturally protect us and our home.

I felt God urging me to take action for the victims of Kaduna during the hours we were able to leave our homes. I began to transport co-workers from the bank back to their houses. If they were unable to return home due to threats, I brought food to the office where they took refuge. My mother and the women staying with us faithfully took food to our neighbors as well. It was not uncommon during the height of the violence for the men to spend their evenings protecting our churches from attack and destruction — I was no exception.

We took advantage of the more peaceful hours getting caught up on sleep, gathering in prayer, worshipping, drawing close to God and reading his word.

Little did I know that across the city of Kaduna, my future wife, Laura, was also experiencing the effects of the '92 riots. Her father was a banker, too. They lived in a large home that could house many. As lovers of Jesus, they felt it necessary to allow as many displaced Christians into their home as possible.

I always chuckle when I hear Laura speak of those days. She will say, "The only way I knew there was any real problem was because I saw the reports on the television. All I knew was we had a lot of friends and relatives staying with us — it was like one big slumber party. There were so many, I could only assume some were friends of friends. There were people sleeping in the hallways and on the floor in every room.

"Because God had blessed us with such a large home, we turned away no one. The Christians living with us told me horror stories of the streets and in the neighborhoods of Kaduna, but I felt very unaffected. They would tell me about homes being burned, how they were stopped by mobs of Muslims and of their thankful hearts toward the police who helped them escape."

Our neighborhood consisted of more Muslims than Christians, and since we lived in the Muslim north, we were at risk to be sucked into the persecution looming around us. I remember my father — and the other men, armed with guns — awake throughout the night keeping a vigilant eye over us. Fortunately, our home had very high fences for security purposes. Between the fences and the men, I felt relatively safe during the crisis.

In the beginning of the lockdown, we were not allowed to leave our homes. Since the government shut down all schools and businesses, the people in our home were together day and night. At one count, we had 45 mouths to feed. That made daily life a bit chaotic. I recall the children screaming and running amok playing chase, tag or any game that would release their pent-up energy. Thankfully, Mom had at least two months of food stored that we could draw from until we could make it to the market. After two or three days, the sanctions became more relaxed, and we were able to venture out for food and supplies during the peaceful hours of the morning.

I prayed each day. Everyone collectively prayed at night before bed. Soon, the bond of those living under our roof strengthened with the power of Christ over us. My longing to pray did not originate from a fearful heart. My prayers came from a heart for my people. The sadness toward my neighbors and community motivated me. I could hardly bear to see strong relationships turn bitter and cold. People spewed threats at one another and burned each other's places of worship down. Trusted friendships dissolved into a pool of confusion glassed over with a sense that no one could be trusted.

As horrifying as the '92 Zangon-Kataf riots were, in retrospect, Laura and I feel fortunate to have lived through them. We were able to see the protection of God over our families and Christians banding together in prayer throughout Kaduna, as well as Christians helping Christians in a joint effort to protect each other's lives.

We are also able to share the lessons of those experiences when we meet people here in Gig Harbor.

తతత

Laura experienced a narrow escape during the 2000 Sharī'ah crisis. You'll want to hear her recount those events for herself.

Laura

I was on my way to work one morning during the dry season in Kaduna. It was a morning like any other with busy rush-hour traffic. I was thanking God for my employment and the beautiful distant scenery when something caught my eye. It appeared to be a peaceful demonstration as Christians chanted from the worn edges of the sidewalks, "No Sharī'ah Law." I saw picket signs with "Freedom from Sharī'ah Law," "John 3:16" and others with cries for help written on them. The sign holders' posture betrayed a hint of worry.

By mid-morning, customers were coming to my counter at the bank whispering anxiously.

"Riots are going on in town. I have to hurry up and get all my banking done. If this turns into a lockdown, there's no telling when I will be able to get back here."

"I'm in a bit of a hurry. I heard churches are being burned and Christians are being killed in downtown Kaduna."

One woman told me, "I am afraid it may be too dangerous for me to get home. What am I going to do? If I meet a mob, I am as good as dead."

By noon, the wrought-iron gates around the bank were locked. This provided me some sense of security, but not enough to pin down my next move. As I observed the events of the afternoon, there was a marked difference from the 1992 crisis — the Muslims were panicked and scurrying to get their business taken care of. They didn't want the roads to their neighborhoods blocked any more than the Christians, nor did they desire to meet a Christian mob on their journey home.

The bank stayed open until 5 p.m., and I chose to see my shift to the end. In fact, many of my co-workers did the same. They were too afraid to go. I had called my brother for a ride home, but I was convinced he would be unable to make it safely. As I loitered in the lobby, I overheard some co-workers talking.

"I think I am just going to stay here until this crisis ends."

"Not me, I'm going out to fight. I'm tired of this. Maybe violence is the best way to solve these problems. Nothing else seems to work."

"Violence is not the answer. I think people on both sides are tired of the fighting and the killing. Don't you?"

"I don't know, but I have to go before it's too late. I don't need to be stopped and killed by a mob of angry Christians after all we have been through today."

I was blessed to find a ride home with a co-worker from my neighborhood that evening since I didn't have my own transportation. The last thing I wanted to do was live in the bank for the next four or five days. I figured it was better to risk driving the back roads home than to be cooped up in that stuffy, sterile bank. I grabbed my purse, along with a few belongings, and we headed into Kaduna.

Just as the door shut behind me, I caught a glimpse of a woman in the lobby staring through the windows as though contemplating whether to go or stay. Her outward fear mirrored everyone's inward emotions.

ৰৈৰৈৰৈ

Ezekiel

God has taken us from coast to coast since we arrived in the United States shortly after getting married in 2001. We are grateful for our church family at Harbor Life Church in more ways than we can count.

We love serving and sharing all we have learned from life's experiences back in Nigeria with anyone who will listen. Jesus continues to teach us, and we submit ourselves to learning his truths each day. We are thankful for all he has done to get us to Gig Harbor. However, we sorely miss our family back in Kaduna State. We are not only worlds apart geographically, but also in our day-to-day struggles.

The headlines from our home country continue to alarm us.

"Boko Haram Gunmen Kidnap 300 Schoolgirls."

"Shiite Suicide Bomber Kills 32 Near Religious Procession."

"Revenge Killings in Kaduna."

Our concern for the safety of our people deepens. Laura's mom told her about an Islamic attacker who disguised himself as a student in a Nigerian boarding school only to detonate a bomb that killed 50 students. His complaint: The school did not teach the Qur'an.

The rise of Boko Haram has become a serious threat. They are a militant Islamist movement based in Northeast Nigeria.

Their name means "Western education is forbidden," and they instigate many current religious crises of today. Several political leaders are supportive of the Boko Haram. Oftentimes, it seems the government is not responding to their attacks. This puts citizens at extreme risk.

Just because we have escaped the violence of everyday Nigerian life does not mean we've turned a blind eye to the progressing momentum of persecution in that area. In fact, it is quite the opposite. We want to bring awareness to how the church of Nigeria is handling the uprisings and challenge American Christians to come together under the power of the Holy Spirit to pray for not only Nigerians, but for one another. There is great power in the church body when we bear one another's burdens through prayer and submission to God.

ॐॐॐ

One morning as I sat across from Laura, she had a glimmer in her eyes. I wondered, *Is it the coffee, or something else?*

She cracked a smile.

"What are you smiling about?"

"Oh, for some reason I keep flashing back to several commercials I watched on the television with the army of people living in my house back in 1992. I remember years afterward, the ladies and I would quote lines from movies we'd watched to pass the time back then. In fact, just the other day, I was talking to Moraya, and we both quoted, in unison, a line from a movie we remembered watching. We couldn't remember for the life of us the name of that movie. Isn't that funny?"

I love her inner joy. I stared at her for a moment before replying, "I'm glad we can look back at those times with laughter. God had a purpose for us living there, and I know he has one for us being here, too."

She looked beautiful as the sunlight from the window highlighted the many colors in her black hair. It inspired me to ask, "What are you most thankful for, Laura?"

She slowly stirred her coffee as she stared out the window pondering the question as if the answer was worth a million dollars. She dawdled a bit longer before looking up to answer, "For our family. You and our kids mean everything to me. Our trip back to Nigeria in 2011 made me thankful we could raise them here, away from the oppression of Sharīʿah law and civil unrest. I have been thinking about Romans 8:28 lately as I reflect over my life. I see how 'God works all things together for the good for those who love him and are called according to his purpose.' He has done that for us, Ezekiel."

She took my breath away with her wisdom, beauty and calmness.

I nodded in complete agreement.

All things, God can work together for good. Even extreme violence like we escaped in Kaduna. All things. For good.

WHAT REALLY MATTERS
The Story of Ethan
Written by Laura Paulus

I looked around the large room.

How did I get here? Had it really come to this?

There were rows of chairs, almost all filled with kids and belongings piled up or strewn about on the floor. I couldn't believe how many people there were. Many looked exhausted and worn out. Some just looked sad. I noticed a few joyful faces, but they were outnumbered by those who looked like life mistreated them.

The number 54 flashed on a screen. The machine that dispensed the paper tickets stood over in the corner. I walked around the kids playing on the floor and stepped up to get my number — 114. It looked like I'd better find a chair and get comfortable.

A chair sat open, sandwiched between a woman with a baby crying on her lap and a man reading a paper. Sitting there with nothing but time and my thoughts, I began to reflect on it all. I realized how much I'd overlooked people going through pain or difficulties, particularly related to financial need. As I looked around, something softened in me. I needed the same thing they did. How quickly a change in circumstances changed my perspective.

I looked down at my slacks and shoes. Good quality — though faded and worn from so much use, they still looked decent. Things could always be worse.

RECALIBRATE

Just three years earlier, my family lived the American dream. We owned a huge home, several nice cars, boats, investment properties and more. My job as a real estate agent provided me with money and a flexible schedule to allow for time to enjoy the things my job afforded us.

Things seemed to change almost overnight. Now we were basically homeless. I resorted to coming into a local welfare office to find a way to feed my family. Here sat people I previously judged for needing welfare.

And there I was, one of those people.

☙☙☙

I was born 15 months after my older brother, Micah, and our sister came along a few years later. We came from a loving family, and I enjoyed a wonderful childhood. My siblings and I loved growing up in our family. We felt supported and loved.

Micah and I were close growing up. He was always a great guy, even when we were competing with each other. I felt proud to have him as my brother. After we went off to college and then moved on in life, we drifted apart simply because we both got busy with our own lives. We knew that we were there for each other if one of us needed anything, but we were anxious to settle into our own routines.

During my attendance at the local community college, I met Gabriella. She walked into one of my classes at the start of the semester, and I immediately noticed her. Our eyes met, and I could see a spark of interest.

"Hey, who was that beautiful girl? Do you know her?"

Word got back to her that I had asked about her. The time came for me to get to know this interesting woman.

I went up to her during our very next class and introduced myself.

"Hi, Gabriella. My name is Ethan."

We quickly became friends. After a few weeks, we both decided we were meant for each other and started dating. After several months, I transferred to the University of Hawaii, as I'd planned before we met. Gabriella and I continued our relationship in spite of the distance between us, but we missed each other. She transferred at the semester break so we could attend the same school.

Our time in Hawaii held a magical element. We got to spend all of our time together in an amazing location. Gabriella and I talked about marriage and what we wanted our marriage to look like. I loved that Gabriella possessed strong opinions about how things should be.

"Ethan, the culture I come from is very male driven. Women typically do not do anything outside the house, including getting a college degree. My dad broke the roles and told me I could go to college and do anything I wanted to do. I was his baby and the only girl, and he always wanted me to know that I could have the world. I have watched marriages around me where the man is in charge and the woman just goes along. I want so much more for us."

"Like what, Gabriella? What do you picture when you think of us married?"

"I want a partnership. I want to do things together, in agreement, and not just do things because it fits the roles we are supposed to play. I want us to be a team."

"I completely agree with that. It is how my parents have always handled their marriage, and I would love to build ours the same way."

We spent hours talking about what our married life together would look like. Neither of us ever doubted that we were meant for each other.

I planned a romantic proposal for her on her 21st birthday while we lived in Hawaii. We decided on a short engagement after we moved back to Washington and lived about a half an hour away from each other. That seemed too far after we had lived just yards away from each other in Hawaii. We were ready to begin our life together.

Three months later, we wed on August 3.

After returning from our honeymoon, I went to work with my dad in the family business as an electrician. I had completed four years of school, but not my degree. My dad needed the help, and I needed the work, so I left school to begin working.

శశశ

Gabriella continued in school and graduated two years after we were married. She received her degree and planned to pursue a career as a history professor. The same month that she graduated from the University of Washington, we realized she was pregnant. Gabriella felt bad that she'd finished her degree while I worked, only for her to end up staying at home with our son, but we both felt the importance of the role of mom far outweighed any outside job she could have. She settled into motherhood and did an amazing job.

Eventually, I became a real estate agent, and we continued accumulating wealth as our family grew. We felt like we were living the good life as we added nice things and healthy children. After three boys, we had a little girl. Gabriella continued to stay home with our kids, and she homeschooled them. We both felt that this worked best for us rather than to send the kids off to school while she worked. And her degree gave her excellent qualifications to educate them.

My earnings were substantial. But so was the debt we accumulated. It seemed like the more I made, the more we spent, and we lived outside our means. It could be exhausting at times trying to balance everything and keep paying for a lifestyle to which we grew accustomed.

We traveled a dangerous path not handling our finances responsibly. And we ultimately suffered the consequences.

ॐॐॐ

In 2007, at 32 years old, I watched the real estate market crash. For several months, we were fine. I continued to make money, although the checks started dwindling down to one or two per year. While they were substantial checks, they fell short of what we needed. The next year, I went for six months without a paycheck, and we started having problems paying the mortgage on our house. I'd bought another house as an investment shortly before the crash. On the weekends, I started fixing it up in case we lost the home we were living in and might need a place to stay. I took about $20,000 out of one of my checks to invest in fixing up the investment house.

That only bought us a little time.

A friend called and told me about a job in a town about two hours away where I could earn good money in the telecom business. While the base pay began at only $24,000, with commissions and bonuses I expected I could easily earn $100,000 to $150,000. It seemed like perfect timing and just what we needed to get out of our financial hole. I possessed no experience in the field, but I was willing to work hard and thought, if I could just get my foot in the door, I could do well. They hired me, and I hit the ground running.

Unfortunately, the job turned out different than I expected. The training barely existed, and the commission structure ended up being very different than the manager stated in the beginning. I made less than $2,000 per month for a year for a family of six, which did not begin to cover expenses or move us forward. I kept at it hoping that maybe after I put my time in and paid my dues, it would get better. I left for work at 5 a.m. and came home at 7 p.m., leaving me little time to see my family.

My confidence began to slip as I felt disappointed

about myself and my lack of success. It is important for a man to feel he can provide for his family. Well, I did everything in my power to do that, and I seemed to fail.

My confidence slipped further when the bank foreclosed on our home and we couldn't move into the other house because it wasn't ready. We borrowed about $90,000 from someone we knew as a hard money loan, attached and recorded as a note and deed of trust with regular payments and an agreed-upon interest rate. We put it toward the investment house, even though it needed about $200,000 worth of work. I continued to attempt to sell real estate to make some money.

Things got out of control quickly.

ॐॐॐ

While my parents raised me in a Christian home, I took our faith for granted. We went to church and attended church camp during the summer, as well as other youth group activities. We even prayed and asked God for things, but we lived a pretty good life, and things were always fine. We did not have big struggles. In fact, I often felt like less than a great Christian since my easy life never contained any big moments of need or crisis. Growing up, I didn't have a strong story about how God turned my life around.

When Gabriella and I began taking our family to Harbor Life Church, we all loved it from the beginning. The kids went from dreading church to gladly getting ready and attending every week. We got involved there and started attending something called a life group in addition to Sunday school and the regular services.

That's when our financial troubles really started building. Another couple in our small group went through the same thing since he worked as a general contractor. He also owned a house going into foreclosure. I called and asked him if we could just move into the house for about two months until we could get back on our feet and get our home repairs finished. He agreed. My friend later told me that his attorney advised him not to let us move in.

"Well, I realize that your attorney is advising you not to let us move in, and you do not want to tell me it is okay and go against him. If I am reading you right, you support this even though you can't say it outright. I don't have a lot of options right now, so I am going to just do it."

"I am so glad this works! I am relieved that you have a place to go. I already lost the house, but at least you can get some good out of it."

"Thanks so much for this. I can't tell you how much it helps."

"Ethan, we help each other out when we can. That is what church family does. I know you would do the same for me."

This man and his family and their home helped us out greatly. While we were sad to give up our huge home, we wouldn't miss the location. Our old neighborhood had no other children. When we moved into the place going into foreclosure, there were neighborhood kids waiting to greet my kids. These kids all grew close. They would run in and out of each other's homes just as comfortable there as in their own places.

We made improvements to the house and, I believe, to the neighborhood that we moved into as well. Even though we were living rent-free, I put time into fixing things in the home. We worked to make improvements. We took pride in the home we lived in, even if neighbors did not understand why we made the effort.

"Hey, neighbor! Why are you painting that? You should just have the owner do it."

"I don't mind. I like working on it."

I couldn't tell him that the owner walked away from the home, and my family and I were living there rent-free. I worried about what the neighbors would all think about that. We had enough stress living day to day, worried that the bank would show up to kick us out and reclaim the house.

It continued to be a struggle to feed my family, let alone pay back the person who'd written us a loan the year before. A month after we moved into our friend's home, we needed to get some financial assistance for food.

So I went one cold February day to the welfare office. As I sat in the chair waiting for my number to be called, I looked around at all of the people sitting there. Maybe because I also needed help, I began to see all of these people and their pain. I mean *really* see them. I saw them how I realized God must see them. These people were no different than me. They probably did not deserve to be in the position they were in any more than I did. Life just happens sometimes.

God loves all of us. He cares about our needs.

What a surreal moment. I began to pray to God as I sat there and saw the needs of those around me. I felt certain that God heard me, and I felt connected to him in a new way.

I realized that trusting God was the only way my family and I could get through all of it. He would get us through — I knew that more than anything since the whole mess started.

As the hits kept coming, I kept asking God to get us through. We gave up the investment home by selling it in a short sale. This involved hiring an attorney to help sort out the whole thing, which only cost more money. My student loans were well past due, so they garnished my wages and took $600 out each month until we hit the point of needing to file bankruptcy.

But there were good moments in the midst of the bad. Something clicked in my heart that day sitting in the welfare office. I firmly believed that a plan and a purpose must exist for all of it. We'd lost several nice cars, but my parents continued to be there for us, and my dad gave us a truck to use.

Our power got shut off during some of the coldest days of the year. We went to stay with my parents. The kids found it a great adventure as we camped out at Grandpa and Grandma's.

They seemed to have little idea we were struggling.

They knew that sometimes things were tight and we had to trust God for everything, but they did not know the extent of our poverty. I borrowed money from a friend to get the power turned back on. Shortly after that, our furnace went out. It cost around $2,000 to fix it, and we did not have anything close to that. We made do without it by using borrowed heaters plugged in throughout the home.

One day, the mailman brought a surprise.

"Ethan, there's a check here for you. It came in the mail."

"A check for what?"

"I don't know," Gabriella said. "Look at it."

I opened the envelope. It came from seven years before when we were in escrow on one of our homes. I handed it over to Gabriella to see.

"Ethan, this is the exact amount for our furnace. This is what we prayed for. God heard us and answered."

"He did. He always comes through, doesn't he?"

Many of our thought processes changed during all of these struggles, but never our faith. No matter how little we made, we always made it. We did have to constantly choose to embrace our faith and trust in God's plan. There were still moments of struggle with that along the way. But God continued to help us.

Gabriella continued to homeschool our children. She struggled with feeling that she was not bringing in income to help out with the bills, and she wondered if she should put the kids in school and get a job. On top of her own thoughts, some of her family pressured her to put her degree to use and help out financially.

"I feel so conflicted and torn with all of the high expectations set for me by myself and my family. I should only care about what you and our kids think, Ethan, but you know my family is very close-knit. I really care what my family thinks about it all."

"What do you want to do?" I asked. "If you want to get a job, I will support you. If you want to stay home with the kids and homeschool them, I will support you."

"As believers, our faith and our finances come from God," she replied, as she turned away from the sink of dishes she was washing and dried her hands. "Trying to take control rather than trusting the Lord to provide and lead us is not the right way to go, and I do not want to do that. My mom was such a great example of this, and she taught me well. I think God wants me to stay home and teach our children about him."

"Could they go to school and still learn about God at home? I think if we know exactly why we are putting them in school or schooling them at home, we will not have to second guess ourselves anymore."

"Putting the kids in school brings other issues up." I pulled up a chair and faced her while she continued. "While I hope that we teach our kids about God in our behavior and conversations, we would become so busy rushing around trying to get four kids to school. And then there are afterschool activities and other things that would take up all of our time. We still have to work hard when homeschooling, but things can be done at a different pace. We can skip to our own beat rather than running around and being stressed."

I thought back to when our oldest two children had been enrolled in their first years of school. She presented a great point.

I couldn't imagine the chaos for us of transporting and scheduling four kids in public school and extracurricular activities.

My insightful wife took a deep breath and continued. "I am also worried about the things that they will learn in school. We can protect them from unhealthy things at home. And we can take charge of their academics. Our kids are learning and doing well on their state tests. They get one-on-one attention from me, an educated teacher. Even in a private school, our kids would not get that much. Not to mention that we cannot afford a private school."

"I don't think we can put a price on our kids getting a quality education while not dealing with extra stresses," I replied. "Any job you find would not make enough to justify putting our kids in school. We have prayed about this, and we both feel this is what God wants for our family. Let's embrace it and learn what he has to teach us through it. We know we can only do this with his help. I trust that this is his plan even if we do not know all of the reasons."

I smiled as I watched the relief flood her face. Our children's education meant so much to her. And I loved that about her. She wanted to do the best thing for them. She wanted to do the best for all of us.

"Yes, I agree completely. This gives me confidence to continue forward with homeschooling our children."

Sometimes, with less than $50 in our checking account, we were clueless as to how we were going to pay our bills or get food for our family. One night, the kids wanted ice cream, so we went to the local ice cream shop. We needed this family time and a bright spot of a treat in the midst of our struggles, so we decided to do it. We ordered everything and went up to pay, trying not to worry about how much it would cost. We believed it was important and trusted God would take care of the details.

"So, how much do we owe?"

"You don't owe us anything. The gentleman ahead of you paid for all of your ice cream."

"What? We don't owe you anything? Why did he pay for us?"

"I am not sure of his reason, sir. The man paid for his ice cream and then asked how much yours was since he wanted to pay for it."

We saw that as yet another example of God looking out for us.

ॐॐॐ

It soon became clear that I could not stay at my job. How could I when it did not give us enough money to live on? We would never be able to get back on our feet unless I brought in more money.

WHAT REALLY MATTERS

I wanted to continue in the telecom field since I enjoyed it, so I applied at another company. The position seemed like my dream job. I progressed through several stages of the hiring process before I got turned down.

Thankfully, another company hired me. New salespeople were given the first six months to ramp up our sales. At the end of the six months, a new boss came on and decided to fire everyone below a certain percentage of sales. I fell just short of it and lost my employment along with 40 other people.

About that time, the guy chosen instead of me at my dream job lost his position. The manager called me and offered me the job. I stayed there as one of their top three sales people for two years. My boss said that he never saw a more positive person. I learned to be a glass-is-half-full kind of guy even in the worst of times. A hard worker, I did not fear giving everything to my work. We started getting ahead, little by little.

When I left that position to begin a higher-paying job, the new salary started allowing us to get ahead and pay off debt. I learned about that opportunity from a contact I made at the first stint I got in the telecom company. It was interesting to see how God brought things full circle. Even though that assignment did not have what I needed or expected, it later led to a great job. All of it became part of the journey that God took us on.

స్తెస్తెస్తె

My wife has been my best friend. We are a team. When I got stressed out and felt like we could not possibly go on, she remained strong and reminded me of God's faithfulness. When she got down, I reminded her that we'd already been through so much and could get through anything.

We also reminded each other to continue to appreciate the little things and the big things. One of our favorite books is *1,000 Gifts*, by Ann Voskamp. The author shares about her journey to find joy in God and to be thankful in everything. It helped us to look for things to be grateful for and to celebrate.

For example, Gabriella wanted a pair of boots for three years that cost more than we could afford. One day she found a pair on Amazon for a fraction of the list price. It fit our budget, and she ordered them. They arrived and, thrilled, she pulled them out and showed them to me.

"Look what God gave me!"

I'd forgotten about how great the little blessings are. "Sweetheart, I don't think God really cares that much about your boots when we have all of these other things going on."

"Don't you take away my blessing that the Lord gave me."

She quietly slipped out of the room and took her boots upstairs. It hit me. *We have been striving to find the joy in everything. We have learned to look for God's plan. And I just threw all that out the window and hurt my wife with my thoughtless words.* I hurried after her.

"You are right. It is not my role to decide what qualifies as a big enough blessing. He meets us in the big things and in the small things. I am really sorry."

"It's okay. I forgive you."

෩෩෩

Money will come and go, but I believe God is the light and the truth and does not change. At one time in my life, I wanted my kids to have the finest things in life. I thought we needed lots of money and belongings, that having wealth could teach them to strive for the best. That mindset changed for me. With a lot of money, I stressed out — always working harder to get more things. My focus fell on the wrong things.

We saw God do so much during our financial struggles, and now we know how easy it is for someone to fall into the situation that we were in. I know we are not the only ones who have gone through financial hardships. I want others going through struggles to see our lives and find hope that it will get better. We are not alone. Everyone, even Christians, goes through trials and tribulations. I tell them, God is there to help.

I believe God knew where our story would go. I believe he put us in the setting of Harbor Life Church with people who would support us and have our backs. It used to be like pulling teeth to get my kids to the services at other churches. At Harbor Life, they love it. They love going every Sunday. We have our church family supporting us.

RECALIBRATE

We did not go to the mall for three years. We did not buy anything there for those three years. We made do with the clothes that we owned, and it worked.

I've begun to pay back student loans again and to work down credit card debt. We live within our means. I paid about $20,000 off in back taxes. We only owe the Internal Revenue Service about $6,000 now and have begun a payment plan to get that done so we can buy a home.

We have been off welfare for two years. I am so grateful that when we needed it, we had it, and I am thankful now that we are done and that it's available for other families who need it.

We have been able to discuss some of the struggles of the past five years with our oldest son. All that God did for us has impacted him. He now goes to high school and feels comfortable talking with classmates about his faith and his beliefs. He can appreciate all that God did through our struggles.

"So all that time, we were broke?"

"Well, we were unable to pay all our bills and often borrowed money just to feed you guys and keep you warm."

"But we have always had food. And a house. And we had lots of fun times with each other. How could we be so poor if we had all of that? I don't remember it."

While we love that our children don't remember all the gory details from those five years, we don't ever want to forget all we went through and learned. They were invaluable lessons.

WHAT REALLY MATTERS

In a short span of time, our family went from *having* some of the finest things in life to really *understanding* the finest things in life — what really matters. We finally understood that family and community mattered more than cars and boats. Experiencing the reality of Jesus' life and love is more important than having a huge home in a prestigious neighborhood. I feel certain I have secured all I need by accepting a personal relationship with God. Money can never buy me that security.

FILLING LIFE'S EMPTY PLACES
The Story of Sheryl
Written by Ruth Ford

If I had written a "to-do list" for that sunny summer Sunday, I would have highlighted two primary items — my 10-year-old daughter's three-on-three basketball tournament and a face-to-face meeting with my half-sister.

That first item was a common, enjoyable occurrence for our family. I didn't become a mom till later in life, and I savored every moment with my three active, athletic children, ages 11, 10 and 7. I relished driving them to and from their various games and tournaments.

In many ways, that Sunday represented just another sports-mom day. Still, I felt a little nervous that morning when my kids and I left our modest home and climbed into our mom-mobile minivan. Soon my kids put in their earbuds so they could enjoy music on the hour-long drive to the park that would host the tournament. That left me plenty of time to consider that second item on the day's schedule — the appointment with my half-sister.

The anticipation brought back a myriad of memories. My life journey had left some empty places inside of me. In spite of that, I chose to be optimistic, looking for the brighter side of circumstances. I would generally describe myself as a positive, joyful person. I often tell my children, "Something good comes out of everything. You can find the negative or find fault — it's your choice. But if you look for the good and look for the joy, you'll find it."

We reached our tournament destination and pulled into the parking lot. Walking to the basketball court where my daughter would compete, we finalized registration details. We watched her tournament and then went to meet my half-sister. I recognized her from her Facebook photos, but I still felt a little overwhelmed.

She looked so much like my biological mom, I almost felt like I was stepping back in time.

ฅ๛ฅ๛

If my life were a movie, and the characters were listed by order of appearance, the first two people would be my dad and biological mom. They both were just 19 years old when my mom gave birth to me. They dated for a year, then my dad joined the Army.

I don't know why, but my mom gave up all rights to me. Since my dad was away, serving in the military, I lived with his mother till I turned 2 years old. That's when my dad returned to get me, and we moved from Idaho to the state of Washington, where he'd found work as an engineer for Boeing. He didn't stay there long, moving on to work as an engineer for a railroad company. But before he left Boeing, he met a woman, and he married her, and she became my mom.

FILLING LIFE'S EMPTY PLACES

After that, my only contact with my biological mom occurred during two-week visits every summer until I reached about 12 or 13 years old. The visits were arranged by my birth mom's mother. She wasn't a stereotypical storybook grandma, knitting or making home-cooked meals and loving on us. She always asked questions like, "How are your grades this year?" Or she would insist, "You must learn to play the piano." And I never wanted to play the piano. She cared about appearances and "who knows who." At some level, I came to see her as a "country club grandmother."

By contrast, my biological mom came across as very warm and outgoing. She was tall with blond hair, blue eyes and fair skin.

Everyone gravitated to her because she was so positive and full of life — always smiling and joyful. During our two-week visits, she often said, "I love you!" Or she said, "I miss you so much!" But outside of those two-week visits, I never heard from her. I didn't even receive phone calls on birthdays or at Christmas.

I never thought she disliked children. After all, soon after she and my dad split, my biological mom married and bore three children. So I always wondered, *Why didn't she want me?*

I kept looking for something to satisfy that hollow feeling.

꙳꙳꙳

RECALIBRATE

My relationship with my stepmom was sort of on and off. In hindsight, I think she did the best she could, given all the circumstances our family faced. As an adult looking back on my growing-up years, the simple fact that she wanted me means a lot. But for whatever reason, it just didn't fill the vacancy in my heart. I kept trying to satisfy that inner longing, and as I got older, I immersed myself in the party scene.

I moved out of my dad and stepmom's house about six months after I graduated from high school, and I lived in an apartment with some friends. But then I ended up moving in with my boyfriend. I lied to my parents about that. I always felt like if I did the so-called right things, they were proud of me. But if I didn't, they were ashamed. I tried to be careful of what I said and did around them, because otherwise I believed I'd let them down. So I kept some information to myself.

My boyfriend, a great guy, often expressed his dreams to me. "I want to get married," he'd say, "and I want to start having kids right away." That scared me. After all, I was only 19 years old. So when I discovered I'd gotten pregnant, abortion seemed like the best option. I found the courage to tell my boyfriend about the baby. He didn't favor me getting an abortion, but he didn't try to stop me.

"I want you to have what you want," he said.

So I went ahead with it.

A friend drove me to the facility, and a nurse showed me into a cold gray office. "Just lie down," she said, pointing toward a table. So I did.

FILLING LIFE'S EMPTY PLACES

She administered some sort of anesthetic, and I became sleepy.

When I awakened, it was over.

My friend drove me back to my boyfriend's house, and I fell asleep. I intentionally blocked the whole experience from my mind, almost like it never happened. But in reality, my abortion created one more empty place that I didn't know how to fill. I found it harder and harder to be happy and okay with who I was, and that hindered my ability to form good relationships.

ҽ∾ҽ∾ҽ∾

A year later, I still lived with my boyfriend, and my life revolved around parties. After work. Weekends. Always. That pretty much summarized my life. I had no goals, no aspirations, no thoughts of anything moving forward in my life. One primary question dominated every moment: "Where's the party?"

One night I joined a group of friends at a local dance club. Colored lights illuminated the dance floor, and a pulsating beat emanated from the disc jockey's speakers. The room was vibrant with energy as dancers twisted and twirled and swayed on the dance floor. I spotted a man who epitomized "tall, dark and handsome." Besides that, he danced well. As I sat on a stool at a round table, he approached and asked me to dance. I said yes.

A friend who accompanied me that night warned me about this particular man. "Stay away from Hugh! He's a womanizer." She attributed several other less-than-positive behaviors to the man, but I laughed her off.

"That just makes him all the more enticing!" Within a short time, Hugh and I were dating, and I finally broke up with my other boyfriend.

By the time I turned 24, Hugh and I were engaged.

෨෨෨

Since I was so heavily enmeshed in the party scene in Tacoma, that's where I met most of my friends. We all sought whatever pleasure we could capture for the moment. I can only speak for myself, but in hindsight, I realize my choices represented my effort to do *something* to avoid facing the fact that my life was aimless, empty and without meaning or purpose.

Then I started noticing one of my friends making some specific changes in her life. I had known her for a couple of years. She was physically very beautiful — tall and thin with dark hair and beautiful skin. Even in a crowd, people noticed her, so eventually we also noticed her absence. She just wasn't partying as much.

"Hey, Kim. There's a big bash at the club on Saturday night. Are you coming?"

Kim paused. "Um — no. I have other plans."

That response became more and more common, and eventually I discovered she was attending church and Bible study.

"I just don't want to keep doing what I've always done. I want a different kind of life," she explained.

FILLING LIFE'S EMPTY PLACES

My mind immediately returned to my childhood experiences at church. Along with my dad and stepmom, I attended a rather stiff and proper church. Our family submitted to a religious system of rules. What to do, what not to do. I don't remember learning much about God, but I do remember the somber music and the repeated standing and kneeling. The congregation of about 200 people gathered in an elegant, ornate building illuminated by a series of chandeliers. Oh, yes — I remember the chandeliers — especially the one that hung over the stairs.

One Sunday when I reached about middle school age, as we ascended to our pew where we liked to sit upstairs, the chandelier started rattling overhead. It fell, glancing off my head, and I required a trip to the hospital for stitches. All these years later, I still bear a scar on my head from that accident.

Since that summarized my experience with church, you can imagine why I was surprised to discover the source of the changes in my friend.

"Church?"

"Yes," she said, nodding. "Would you like to join me?"

Now, that was a new concept for me. Accompany Kim to church? "Sure," I said. "I guess I don't have anything better to do."

So that's how I ended up at church that Sunday. I have to say, this church didn't fit my expectations, based on previous experiences. A huge crowd filled the bright auditorium. The environment was simple rather than elegant, and I sensed excitement and energy from the moment I walked in. A group of musicians played a series of upbeat and joyous songs. When they finished, a man walked to the center of a stage.

He talked about God's incredible love for people. He explained that at some point, all of us have chosen to follow our own way rather than God's. We've let habits come into our lives that displease and even grieve God. But he also explained that God is always reaching toward us, wanting to welcome us. "In fact," he said, "God made a way through his son, Jesus, for our relationship to be restored. Perhaps you're not satisfied with what you've made of your life. If you want something different — if you want to ask Jesus to change you — why don't you come up here to the front and pray with someone?"

I felt like someone lifted me right out of my chair. It's hard to explain, because it wasn't really like a hand pushing from behind me. It felt more like the sensation you get on a roller coaster, when you crest the first hill and then you're propelled downward. Obviously, the actual movement didn't happen that fast, but it was that kind of experience. I walked forward about 10 feet without even realizing it. I didn't look back over my shoulder to see who or what pushed me. I just kept striding forward. Suddenly I stood at the front of the auditorium, and I started sobbing. I felt a rush go through my whole body, almost like a heat wave, signaling an accompanying inner shift in my heart.

I can't say everything changed in my life immediately after that church experience. I still attended services, but not regularly. I went ahead and married Hugh, ignoring the warning signs about his lifestyle. I should have paid attention. Hugh was a workaholic, he gambled and he drank heavily. Eventually, I realized he was having affairs as well. I drew back, realizing I desired something different for my life.

Our only real connection was the business we owned together. Our seven-year marriage was a farce. It didn't fill any empty places inside of me. Instead, it dug more of them. By the time I turned 31, we divorced. I remember those years as a big blur with nothing positive other than our sporadic attendance at a church in Tacoma. That may have been motivated by a sense of obligation rather than true desire to know God better. Still, those times of worship fed my desire for a different lifestyle and a renewed relationship with God.

The one good thing I kept in that experience was my friendship with Kim.

క్రాక్రాక్రా

After the divorce, I worked for an advertising company. I worked with a lot of managers, including a man named Dean. He had a wife and two children, but he let me know his marriage didn't make him happy.

Dean started asking me out.

"Absolutely not!" I replied. "I'm not dating a married man! My life is already a mess, so I'm not going to add that to it."

RECALIBRATE

Shortly afterward, however, Dean and his wife split up, and he asked me to a Seattle Mariners' baseball game. I enjoyed the game, and I enjoyed his company, but I didn't feel any particular sense of attraction to him. Nevertheless, he continued to pursue me, and we started talking on a more personal level.

That's when I started noticing how he talked about his kids. For quite a while, I had wanted to be a mom, and from his comments, I could see him as a great dad. That doesn't mean I saw him as some sort of "ticket for becoming a mom." I just saw him as very genuine. I felt a little nervous about being a stepmom, since I'd been on the other end of that dynamic in my own childhood. But I started noticing that Dean and I shared a lot in common, especially in our life goals.

One evening, as we talked on the phone, Dean made a seemingly off-hand comment. "You know, I really believe a man's wife should be his number one priority." When he said that, I felt a new sense of peace growing inside of me. I felt very safe.

Then one night, as Dean left my townhouse, he said, "I have to ask you something before I leave."

"What is it?" I held my breath.

"Don't you think it's about time we got married?"

I said yes.

ৡৡৡ

FILLING LIFE'S EMPTY PLACES

Within a few years we settled in a coastal community on Puget Sound in Washington, a short distance from Tacoma via the Narrows Bridge. Soon our family included two toddlers, and I filled my life with all the activity that goes with parenting youngsters. Our busy schedule did not include church. I sometimes felt the nudges of memories from my 20-something years, recalling the church where I responded to the message of God's welcoming embrace. Those twinges reminded me that I wanted my children to know about God's great love.

I still chatted by phone with my friend Kim, whose life journey included some rocky pathways. She endured a difficult divorce. For a while she lived in a friend's garage by herself without her children, and she was anxious and fearful for her children's futures. I watched her turn a complete 180 degrees, to the point that if you selected one characteristic to describe her, it would be peace. I knew it came from her relationship with God, and I thought, *I want that, for myself and for my family.*

I also discovered later that Kim prayed for me regularly, and I believe God answered those prayers, because one day I finally decided to take action on that desire for a different kind of life. I found the phonebook, turned to the listings for preschools, took out my phone and punched in a number.

A female voice answered. "Hello. How can I help you?"

"Hi, I'm Sheryl. I'm interested in getting some information about your preschool." I discovered I was talking to the preschool director, so I asked all kinds of questions about availability and assessments. Then, before I set an appointment, I asked a pointed question. "Oh, by the way, this is a Christian preschool, isn't it?"

She laughed and assured me, "Yes, it is."

I didn't experience an irresistible urge like the one that pushed me to the front of the auditorium at the meeting I attended with Kim. I didn't see fireworks or hear a sonic boom. I just made a simple phone call. I wanted my children to enjoy the God who welcomed me when I was in my 20s, so I sought a place offering that opportunity. I'm not sure I realized how much that call would change my life as well as theirs.

I live in a seaside community. People who navigate on the water know that even a small course change, followed over time, can take you to a very different destination. In my life journey, that phone call represented a course change. I came to realize that if I wanted to help my children respond to God, I had to know him better myself.

I started by enrolling my oldest child in that preschool, and then my second child. When we had a third child, I enrolled him there as well. The preschool was part of a Christian elementary school where my children continued their studies. Eventually I started working there. Through our long-term involvement, I met a whole group of Christian women who welcomed me and nurtured my budding trust in Jesus. I started attending a group called MOPS (Mothers of Preschoolers), and in the company of Christian moms I met there, I read the Bible and learned more and more about God. I started talking to him regularly and relating to him as a friend. In that environment, where I felt a sense of welcome and belonging, I responded to what I learned through Bible study and also through the example of the women around me.

One of those moms invited me to her church, and I loved it and felt very much at home there. But that church required a lengthy commute, and it didn't have a very active children's ministry, which became increasingly important as our children grew older.

෴෴෴

During our marriage, Dean launched his own business, and because of his hard work and expertise, we enjoyed tremendous financial gain. We added two rental houses to our holdings, and we signed a contract on a huge 6,400-square-foot house that even had an elevator. On paper, we could afford all of that. Soon after we bought the large house, though, our local economy experienced a downturn, and through a series of unexpected and unfortunate events falling in succession like dominoes, our family lost everything — the business, big house and rental properties. We moved into a modest rented home, and my husband sank into a deep depression.

People say, "Don't wait till something bad happens to look for God." But as I came to realize, he's always there, in the bad times as well as the good. Everything that happened pushed me closer to God rather than propelling me away from him.

I felt like I would crumble if I wasn't around people who believed in Jesus, so I continued surrounding myself with Christian friends. The people I knew from the school my children attended became like family, surrounding and encouraging me, getting me through difficult situations.

We were still attending the church some distance away, but I wished more and more that we could find a place geared toward children and youth. I heard about several different churches, and I visited a few of the really big ones, but I felt lost there. Then someone invited us to Harbor Life. I enjoyed the lively music in the auditorium and the informal atmosphere of the coffee area. I appreciated the well-designed area for children. I liked the children's ministry balance of Bible and worship and play time and games.

Almost immediately, Harbor Life felt like family. I introduced my husband and three children to Pastor Tyson Lash, and he never needed to ask for our names even once after that. I loved the fact that people remembered our names and missed us when we weren't there. The youth pastors even asked for a copy of my kids' sports schedules, because they wanted to support my children in their areas of interest.

We also joined a life group that met twice each month. Everyone brought some sort of food to share, and we ate dinner together. Then the adults all stayed in one room, and the children went elsewhere to play. My kids loved it.

FILLING LIFE'S EMPTY PLACES

They were always asking me, "Is this the Friday night that we get to go to church?"

When my husband found a new job, his depression began to fade. I had already been baptized when I was in my early 20s and made my initial commitment to Jesus. Eventually my husband and three children decided to be baptized at Harbor Life, giving public expression to their relationship with Jesus.

≈≈≈

In the midst of that financially difficult time, a family member let me know my stepmom had been ill, and her diagnosis was cancer. I hadn't really talked to her for about a year. We hadn't fought. We just sort of drifted. Our relationship had always been on and off, and I always felt better if I simply kept my distance. But the "C-word" introduced a new reality into our relationship.

I picked up the phone and called my mom and dad's house. We met first at the hospital, where my mom was enduring some medical tests. When I entered her room, I found my dad there, too. He hugged me. We all talked for the first time in a year. That visit kicked off a series of conversations that continued over the next 10 months before she passed away. We talked almost daily and forgave one another for long-buried issues. I shared different books with her that had encouraged me in finding God's plan for my life journey. We talked almost daily about prayer and believing and not giving up. Those conversations were precious.

Finally, when I visited her one day, I asked her to let me pray with her. She repeated the prayer after me, expressing her desire to have a close relationship with Jesus and to trust him in all circumstances.

"Mom," I said. "I'm so proud of you. I know where you're going."

Mom did pass away, but not before our relationship was mended, so another empty place disappeared in my heart.

And then, after some time, I received a message via Facebook. My half-sister Julie had found my profile. She lived just about an hour away from me.

We communicated via computer for a while, mostly chatting to one another about our kids. Then one day I realized my 10-year-old daughter's upcoming three-on-three basketball tournament was slated for a park very close to where Julie lived. I left her a message saying we would be in the area. She happened to be going to church that morning, and she said, "I'd love to get together after church." She met us at the tournament site.

It was a gorgeous, sunny, warm Sunday, and Julie and I and my three kids wandered for a bit together, taking in the sights and sounds and smells of a local farmer's market hosted that day at the park. We ate lunch and talked, then bought some jars of jam and talked some more. We treated ourselves to coffee. Sitting on the grass together, we continued chatting.

All in all, Julie and I visited for about two hours. Somewhere during that conversation, she asked me to answer a question I'd been asking all my life. Tears were very near the surface for both of us when she asked, "Why were you never in our lives?" I'd always wondered if my siblings even missed me. Now, at least, I knew my sister did.

I took a deep breath.

I'd learned a lot since I started trusting God.

And I believe that trust and faith in God's love allowed me to give her this answer: "I don't know why. But I can tell you this much — life hands you some things you just don't forget, but that doesn't mean you can't forgive. I don't have any ill feelings toward our mom, and I don't want you to have them, either."

And I knew that with God's help, another empty place had been filled.

DON'T WORRY
The Story of Esther
Written by Rosemarie Fitzsimmons

The baby's kick made me smile.

I hummed as I put away the last of the breakfast dishes. My due date was fast approaching, but I could still manage my work around the house. The little guy hadn't seemed active for a few days, so his movement reassured me all was well.

Meanwhile, a doctor across town was frowning over my latest blood test results.

My husband, Leonard, sat at the table nursing the last of his coffee when the phone rang beside him. He answered it.

"Hi, Leonard, it's Doc Wilson. What are you doing?"

"Gettin' ready to go to work. I gotta get that tractor running if I expect to till the garden this weekend."

"No, you're not." The doctor's tone made Leonard sit up straight. "You're going to bring your wife to the hospital. She's having a baby today."

We didn't question, but headed out right away. Whatever the doctor's reason, I trusted he knew what he was doing. When we arrived at the hospital, we found out that the blood test indicated our baby was not receiving nourishment. They had to get him out immediately.

No wonder he seemed sluggish …

I'd already expected to undergo a cesarean section.

RECALIBRATE

Doc Wilson had recommended it because I was more than 40 years old. For the same reason, he'd told me to get an amniocentesis, but I'd refused. No matter what the results might have been, I wanted this baby. And I figured, if the test showed anything wrong, it's not like I could have changed anything, anyway.

The delivery room teemed with activity. I'd never experienced so much attention. The next thing I knew, I was looking into Marvin's sweet hazel eyes. Leonard came in to see his boy, but he'd hardly said hello before one of the nurses whisked Marvin away. That's when we noticed the delivery room was not all smiles and congratulations.

Something was wrong, but nobody would tell us what.

Instead, when the hospital released me, we went home without our son. I returned daily to visit. After two weeks of unbearable waiting and seemingly endless testing, we finally learned the diagnosis.

ॐॐॐ

For the first eight years of our marriage, Leonard and I were content not to have children. As the oldest girl of 10 siblings, I'd pretty much had my fill of taking care of young ones long before I even grew up myself.

My mom and dad were followers of Jesus who raised their seven boys and three girls to honor God and revere him always. We were all born at home except for an 11th child, who was delivered at the hospital but died the same day. Each of us was named for a Biblical figure, a missionary or a preacher. Mom had a missionary's heart and would have loved to travel to foreign lands to help wherever there was need, but her 10 children kept her busy enough in Tacoma, Washington. So instead, she prayed that her children would become missionaries and instilled in us a sense of service that has since passed through the generations. She and Dad prayed for us continuously. Many of their children and grandchildren did become missionaries, as well as preachers, doctors and military men.

I, however, went right off to work at the Boeing factory. While that may sound a little backward, like a departure from my siblings' paths, that's okay. I talk backward, too, sometimes. I tell anyone who wants to listen that I was born that way — backward. I was a breech baby, and I'm proud of that.

So I entered the factory right out of high school as a mechanic, assembling aircraft parts. Eventually I transferred to an administrative position. I stayed at Boeing for 13 years.

I met Leonard at church. He was a soldier at the time at nearby Fort Lewis. We married when I was 25, and he found a job at the local chemical plant. Leonard had 19 brothers and sisters. When we didn't get pregnant, that was quite all right with us — for a while.

After eight years, we concluded I just wasn't going to have a baby, so we looked into adoption. We learned of a baby who was about to be born in Everett, a town about 65 miles north, and leapt at the opportunity to adopt her.

RECALIBRATE

We named her Joy, because that's what she brought to us. She was less than a week old when we met her in Everett. We fell in love right away and made arrangements with her caregiver to come pick her up a few days later. Such a sweet little gal. We thought she'd be an only child.

I left Boeing, and we bought a farm in Gig Harbor where we raised cows, rabbits and chickens. We sold milk, eggs and rabbits. As tough as it was, I enjoyed the work. Leonard was a hard worker, yet he had the worst luck with machinery. Something was always breaking down — the tractor, the farm truck, the wagon — and he'd have to fix it before he could get on with his chore for the day. His temper would flare, but I always found it somewhat funny.

So there I was with a 9-year-old daughter, a husband, a farm and a full life, but somehow, I felt alone. Joy was an independent spirit, and although I loved her dearly, I didn't feel as if she needed me for anything aside from basic provisions. Leonard kept himself busy on the farm, and we seemed to spend more time apart than together. I know it sounds strange, but I think I wanted a companion.

I suppose what happened next was an answer to a prayer I didn't pray, except in my heart.

❦❦❦

Esther, you're going to have a baby.

I sat upright, looking around to see who had spoken, knowing nobody had.

Where did that thought come from?

DON'T WORRY

Around me, members of the congregation acted as if nothing had happened. They nodded and smiled as the preacher gave his sermon. I was paying zero attention to him — I was about to start an argument.

I looked out the window and thought back as hard as I could.

Oh, I don't think so.

But the words came back again. *Esther, you're going to have a baby.*

By that time, I was pretty certain that somehow this was God, so I continued my side of the conversation.

I can't have a baby. I'm 42. Who in their right mind has a baby at 42?

The congregation laughed at something the pastor said, but I could not pull away from this unusual conversation in my head. I just kept staring at the trees outside and thinking.

God, you've blessed us with a wonderful daughter. That's plenty. We don't want another child, thank you.

But the insistent voice would not be swayed.

It's not your decision.

It was no use arguing. How could I argue with God?

I responded with the only words I believed he wanted to hear.

Yes, Lord, fine. I will have this baby.

I didn't discuss this with anyone. Who would believe me, anyway? Over time, I pushed the conversation out of my mind and forgot about it. For nine months.

RECALIBRATE

❧❧❧

"You okay?" My brother Paul looked concerned. He set down the plate he'd carried from the table and stood beside me.

"Just a little nausea. It seems to happen every evening." I gripped the counter ledge until the feeling ebbed.

Paul, also my pastor, visited often and knew I was rarely ill.

"You'd better get to the doctor."

Two days later, I was sitting in the doctor's office listening to his diagnosis.

"Esther, you're pregnant."

"Ha! That's a good one!" I laughed.

"Suit yourself." He turned around and shrugged.

I stared at his back as realization set in. He wasn't kidding.

Of course, I was pregnant.

Whoever heard of evening sickness?

I had to giggle at the backwardness of it.

I found Doc Wilson, an obstetrician, and I started making regular visits. Early on, he said, "I have you underlined in red as a C-section."

Apparently, just as I'd tried to explain to God, I was a tad old to be having a baby.

Doc Wilson also wanted me to undergo an amniocentesis test to make sure nothing was wrong with the baby.

I said, "Doc, the Lord asked me to have this baby, so I will not get that test."

DON'T WORRY

Somehow, I believed that if God was going to give me a child, he would make it a healthy, normal baby. Besides, if my baby had any problems, it would not have changed anything for me. I accepted that God's ways are not my ways.

❧ ❧ ❧

When Marvin was born eight months later, the doctor kept him in the hospital for two weeks to run tests. He'd originally shown indications of heart problems, and the doctor thought they might be permanent. I prayed every day for healing. At the end of the two weeks, Marvin's heart was healed.

But there was another concern, the doctor said. He waited until all tests were complete, and he ruled out all other possibilities. When he was certain, he gave us the news: Marvin had Down syndrome.

I couldn't believe it at first. I figured if God wanted me to have a baby, he'd give me a healthy one. I wasn't angry. Surprised, I guess. But by then, I was already in love with Marvin, so he was perfect as far as I was concerned. Leonard had a bit more trouble with the news, but he was smitten, too. Perhaps that's why God made us wait those two weeks.

Paul dedicated Marvin to the Lord during a church ceremony a few months after Marvin was born. I believe the Lord has watched over him every moment of every day.

RECALIBRATE

I started praying over Marvin right away. In many ways he was a normal boy. I can remember him in church when he was just an infant. One of his favorite activities was hair pulling. The only way we could make him drop a shock of hair was to tug his own until he stopped. It took a few months, but he got the idea.

Marvin required a series of physical therapy visits and a lot of prayer to help his muscles develop. Once he figured it out, he ran the heck out of his little walker. He never learned to speak clearly, but his mind is sharp, and he can make himself be understood. He understands nearly everything people say to him.

One of the hardest things I ever had to do was put Marvin on a school bus when he was old enough for special needs classes. That day marked the first time in my life that I worried and was the start of what would become a lifelong battle in which worry triumphed a lot more than it should have.

The moment Marvin stepped on that bus, oh my, did he wail. I can still picture his little face pressed up against the window, sobbing as the bus pulled away. By the third day I could hardly stand it, imagining him crying all the way to school. I asked the bus driver if there was anything I could do to help her.

"Marvin? That boy's fine." She snapped her gum and grinned. "He stops crying about two blocks from here, happy as a clam."

"Really?" I could hardly believe it. "Is he doing that for my benefit?"

DON'T WORRY

"Must be." Her eyes twinkled with laughter. "Marvin loves going to school."

I felt a little foolish but greatly relieved. Still, worry started to take up the biggest chunk of my days. As long as I was with Marvin, I didn't worry, but the moment he was out of my sight, anxiety kicked in.

What if he's hurt? What if the kids pick on him? What if he gets lost?

I reminded myself constantly that he was in good hands and that the staff members were well trained to do their jobs. The Bible says to take all our worries to God, so I prayed, "Lord, you gave him to me, he's your child. You know I can't be with him every minute. You've got to take care of him."

Whenever I prayed that prayer, I felt relief. For a little while. Within a few weeks or so, I'd be back to worrying. *What if his teacher is a monster?* I'd heard horror stories about special education classrooms. So I prayed, "Lord, the teachers just *have* to like him."

And they did. All his teachers were wonderful. Once in high school, when another child rushed forward to hit the teacher, Marvin stepped in the middle and took the blow himself. He was always protecting people.

I also had to learn that I could leave him with his sister and not worry. To this day, Joy tells a story of the time Leonard and I left home for a while, leaving Marvin with her and their cousin Lynn. Marvin went into the kitchen and started pressing the ice dispenser lever on the refrigerator. He just stood there, hand on the lever, watching ice slide onto the kitchen floor. Lynn came in just as he was tiring and took over, holding the lever until the entire ice bucket was empty. Then the two of them played in the ice, sliding over the floor and giggling until they had their fill. They cleaned it all up before we returned.

But my biggest worry was that one day Marvin would take off and we'd never find him. He often decided in the middle of the night to just leave the house. He'd get dressed, sneak out and start hiking down the highway.

The police called us at 2 a.m. one time.

"Is Marvin Bray your son?" Marvin always carried his identification card.

"Yes, he is."

"Well, we found him over here at the high school, waiting to get in. We'll bring him to your house."

Another time, someone who knew Marvin saw him walking along the road and brought him home. Turns out, he'd been heading to church. That would have been a tougher walk. The school was only a couple miles away, but the church was across town.

One night I peeked into his room, and he was gone. I called 911 and everyone I could think of. Friends and family all over town started looking for him. Finally, one of our neighbors found him on his porch. He'd packed his sleeping bag and all sorts of supplies for the outing and just settled down to sleep there.

Someone might have thought he was trespassing and shot him.

DON'T WORRY

I prayed, "Lord, help him settle down."

And he did, when he found a new outlet for his energy: Special Olympics.

Marvin enjoyed sports, particularly the opportunity it provided for him to be around so many people. It took a few years to find his niche. He decided after the first year that he didn't like track and field, so he tried swimming, basketball, then baseball. He liked them all, but soccer is his passion. Every June, he plays on the local Special Olympics soccer team.

It was a relief to see Marvin interact with others. He enjoyed people in general, and everyone seemed to like him. We've all learned from watching Marvin. Leonard learned to be more patient and understanding. It was no use being angry at Marvin — he didn't understand. So Leonard had no choice but to soften his ways. Marvin brought a gentle peace into our home.

My entire family loved Marvin, and he loved them. One Christmas, however, he had his fill of family. We were celebrating far into the night, and he'd had enough. He went into his room and came back out wearing his pajamas.

"Ever-body OUT!" He stomped his foot. "Go home!"

I still worried over Marvin, although time and time again God showed me that he would be fine.

I sensed the Lord telling me, *Let me take care of the worry, Esther. You just love him.*

Many times over the years, I've tried to obey. I tried to turn everything over to God for him to deal with, and it always gave me relief to do so. Still, I always managed to take it all back again.

လလလ

Leonard began to get sick. He'd worked at a chemical plant for many years, and his lungs were badly damaged. When we realized he wouldn't be able to work the farm much longer, we started planning a gradual transition to our new home. Every step required prayer and patience. As with many special needs people, Marvin didn't take well to sudden change. He was then in his early 20s, but his perspective was still childlike.

Not only would we have to sell the farm, but we also had to consider Marvin's future, as Leonard and I would not always be around to care for him. As we prayed, it became apparent that we needed to find him a group home.

There was a place nearby where Marvin knew many of the residents from his school days. He also knew the man in charge, so we started by going to the home regularly for meals. Then Marvin spent the night there. Then two. Then three. Eventually he moved in, but he always came to stay with us on the weekends.

The staff at the home loved Marvin. The doctors struggled with one girl at the home, trying to stabilize her medication. When she was off balance, she'd become violent and lash out at the women on the staff. Marvin would always put himself between the girl and the women, just as he did with his high school teacher. They came and told me after each incident, "Marvin saved us again!"

Once Marvin became a permanent resident at the group home, Leonard and I started talking to a realtor about buying a new home for us. At first, our options appeared dismal. The homes we looked at were too big, too small or in dire need of repair. Again I turned to prayer.

Lord, if you want us to move, you've got to help us find the right place. I've got to know when I see the house.

The realtor came over the next day and set a flyer on my kitchen table. I knew in my heart I was looking at our new home, and I asked to see it. The moment we walked into the model home, I felt such peace and certainty. I turned to Leonard and said, "This is it."

We signed all the paperwork, and construction on our house began. It would take nearly a year to complete.

The most difficult part of our transition loomed before us: selling our 16-acre farm. It was almost like part of the family. We'd planted vegetables but harvested memories — of children and grandchildren (ours and our siblings') climbing over tractors, learning to drive on the farm truck, tending to the animals and exploring every inch of the place. When we announced our plans, the family was in tears.

"We simply can't do the work." My voice wavered. "We have to sell it. I don't want this place falling down around our ears."

When we didn't find a buyer right away, I prayed,

God, if you gave us this house, you've got to help us sell the farm.

And he did. A year later, just as our new home was nearly finished, a young couple with a 10-year-old boy purchased the farm.

It took a while to settle into our new home. We moved our belongings gradually. I didn't know it at the time, but I believe God had set all these events into motion for me. Leonard would not be living long in the new home.

❧❧❧

When Leonard's health took an even sharper turn downward, doctors put him on oxygen to help him breathe, and he spent his final weeks in and out of the hospital. I wasn't sure how Marvin would react to the hospital scene. Many years earlier, when Marvin was in his late teens, my mom had been hospitalized. I brought Marvin to the hospital with me to see her. I had to forcibly pull Marvin into Mom's room. He was terrified throughout the visit, and I wondered if he could possibly remember his frequent hospital trips when he was an infant. I never figured it out, and I wasn't sure what to expect this time, so I prayed he would be okay.

Marvin sat for a long time with his father in the hospital, seemingly unaffected by whatever nightmares he'd experienced in the past. I know his presence brought peace to Leonard in those last days. Then it was time to call Leonard's family in Colorado to come say goodbye.

DON'T WORRY

People arrived from everywhere, and as activity began to pick up, my nephew took Marvin back to the group home. I was glad he didn't have to be there when Leonard died.

I went to the group home and sat down with Marvin to explain that Dad was in heaven with Jesus. I could see his mind working, but I didn't know how much he understood about death.

After Leonard's funeral service, we all went to the cemetery. A grounds worker came to me and said, "Um, ma'am, we have a problem. The backhoe broke down. We'll have to fix it before we can bury him."

"That's fine." I couldn't help laughing. He must have thought I was nuts. "Leonard's used to this." I knew that if Leonard were watching, he'd be laughing as well. What a perfect way to say goodbye to someone who had to fix everything before he could use it.

When the backhoe was ready, some of the mourners walked to the grave site. I drove, watching Marvin (who was one of the pallbearers) with pride as he walked up front with the director. After a very nice graveside service, Marvin said goodbye. He took his father's death well, I thought.

We brought home the picture we'd had made of my husband for the service and hung it in the living room. For a long while after that, Marvin would come in and just stare at the picture, and he'd talk to it. He carried a smaller picture of his dad with him all the time.

RECALIBRATE

ತ್ತಾ ತ್ತಾ ತ್ತಾ

After my husband died, I knew in my heart I wanted to continue caring for people. What better place for meeting new people than at the YMCA? I attended regularly to exercise, and I met many friends. Eventually I started to pray with them. The choir director from the volunteer YMCA choir came to me and said she felt ill, so I prayed for her. A few days later she came back and said, "Esther, since you prayed for me, I am fine."

Then it became routine.

"I'm going to have eye surgery."

"So and so is sick."

"My grandson is in trouble."

"Of course," I'd say. "Let's pray!"

We'd stop what we were doing and just sit out in front of the Y, praying. The staff became accustomed to seeing us there with our heads bowed. I have a list of my Y friends and pray for them every day.

Although I've learned to pray unceasingly, particularly after all God has done for me, my faith isn't always as strong as one might think. I find extra strength in our family prayer gatherings. My siblings and I meet at my place every Monday afternoon for a potluck dinner, and we pray for our family, just as our mother and father prayed for us. In recent years our prayers have been addressing illness and ushering family members off to be with the Lord.

DON'T WORRY

ৰ্কৰ্কৰ্ক

My heart became heavy when my two youngest brothers were suffering with cancer. The second-youngest, Wesley, had served in Vietnam. He didn't go to church for a long time after he returned. Then he developed cancer, which we believe stemmed from contact with Agent Orange, and while he was in the hospital for chemo treatment, he said he believed he heard God say he was going to be healed.

I walked to his hospital room despondent, not really wanting to witness Wesley in his last days. My faith was low. I could barely muster a smile.

Wesley's pastor stood by his bed, and they were talking about the healing power of God. Wesley's face beamed when he saw me.

"God's going to heal me, I know it!"

Something in his voice lifted me. I listened to the two of them talk and felt my faith increasing just by being there. Wesley went into remission. He started attending church every Sunday and loved to say he loves the Lord.

My youngest brother, Timothy, had thyroid cancer. The doctor told him he had just a few weeks to live, but he kept a positive attitude about healing. He went into remission for quite a while, then the cancer returned.

We stood by him, prayed for him and supported him. His son is the youth pastor at his church and had the opportunity to read the first draft of this story to him. He hung on through Christmas with his family and died just after the New Year in 2015.

RECALIBRATE

Through the years, I've prayed for Marvin's health. My father died of a heart attack, and my mother died of cancer. Since then, heart problems and cancer have been prevalent in our family. Sometimes we beat it, and other times we don't. My brothers have all had heart issues, many have stents implanted and all have kidney stone problems. So far, Marvin has been disease-free, and I thank God for that continually. Marvin has regular checkups so that if anything does happen, we'll catch it early.

છે છે છે

In 2012, I had to explain to Marvin that his aunt and uncle had both gone to live with his dad in heaven. It looked like he understood, and he was sad, but his greatest blow came with the death of a good friend at the group home.

Benjamin had been wheelchair-bound and unable to speak. His death was such a shock, the staff at the group home called me over to explain to Marvin what happened. After Benjamin's funeral, Marvin came to me with the program that had his friend's picture on it. He'd been to enough funerals by then to know what the program meant. He was sobbing so woefully it nearly broke my heart.

"Oh, my dear." I pulled him to me and rocked with him. "Benjamin is much better off now. In heaven, Benjamin can walk, and he can talk. And you know how he loved his music? He can always listen to music now."

134

DON'T WORRY

Marvin couldn't seem to bounce back after Benjamin's death. I prayed that God would help Marvin heal, and he did. When Marvin went with his work crew from the group home to San Diego for a three-day vacation, he had a wonderful time, and the distraction was just what he needed. He doesn't carry his pictures of Dad or Benjamin anymore, and he doesn't stare at Leonard's photo on the wall as often.

తతత

Of all the prayers I've ever said over Marvin, I prayed most fervently that he would somehow know who Jesus is and understand how much Jesus loves him. I've seen plenty of evidence that God answered that prayer as well. Anyone who walks into Harbor Life Church will notice him right away, sitting in a front pew, praising the Lord with everything he has. He sings and dances and raises his arms in abandon. Marvin loves God, his church and Pastor Tyson so wildly, other church members have come to tell me they've been blessed just watching him.

We both love Harbor Life Church. The people are very friendly. You walk in and feel at home. Marvin even serves as a greeter at the door sometimes. He has a wonderful time.

Most people have learned how to interpret the way he talks, and he also uses universal gestures. I have to watch him, though — he will go up and start conversations with anyone. Some senior citizens and visitors can have trouble understanding him, and I have to intervene. He also has no hesitation about hugging people, even strangers. He's such a good-hearted young man.

❧❧❧

Has all this allayed my worries? I wish I could say yes, but I still struggle. Sometimes I worry about how Marvin will handle life's curve balls when I am not around. I'm trying to work on my will. *How can I make decisions about Marvin? What if I make the wrong decision?*

Pastor Tyson said you just make the right decision and leave it to God. So once again, I try to hand my worries over to the Lord.

You put Marvin here, Lord. I'm expecting you to take care of him.

And I do believe he will.

❧❧❧

That day in the delivery room when Marvin was born, I didn't understand, but I had peace knowing God knew what he was up to. Marvin was a blessing to my husband, who needed to learn patience and gentleness. I can still picture the two of them dressed up in their finest for my nephew's wedding. They were quite a pair.

But if I asked God for the real reason Marvin was born, I believe he would say he sent Marvin for me. Even today, whenever my boy sees me, his eyes light up, and he runs over to give me a hug (yes, sometimes extra-big, excruciating hugs, but I love them). Marvin has been a blessing in disguise — a true companion and a source of constant joy, someone who reminds others to notice and take joy in the world around them.

Marvin brings his computer tablet to church every Sunday and takes pictures with it constantly. We once had to admonish him not to take pictures during the service, and he obliged. I'd say he has a couple thousand pictures of himself stored on that machine. He delights in them, and I do believe he sees himself the way God does. I often think the rest of us are the disabled ones and that we can learn a lot about life by watching Marvin.

I learned a song in children's church that has stuck with me all my life. It reminded me to pray instead of worry through the difficult times.

Why worry when you can pray?
Trust Jesus, he'll be your stay.
— *by John W. Peterson*

PUSHING THROUGH
The Story of Dr. John VanDruff
Written by Arlene Showalter

"Am I dead?" I tried to open my eyes, but the lids refused. Finally, they cooperated enough for me to take in my surroundings. White walls. White ceiling. White sheets. Machines clacked and whispered and twittered about me.

I tried to lift my head. It remained on the pillow in stubborn defiance. My body felt like sacks of waterlogged grain.

Mom's face came into view of my limited vision. *Mom? Where am I, and what are you doing here?*

I opened my mouth, but only a parched grunt pushed past my numbed lips.

"Relax, John." She laid a hand on my arm.

"What?"

"You had an accident."

છે છે છે

The world was on the brink of war, and the Great Depression still ravaged our nation in 1936, the year I was born in the Midwest. My first major challenge in life came in the form of an alcoholic father who punctuated angry words with clenched fists. He stumbled out of our lives when I was 7, and Mom moved us — without Dad — to Arizona.

RECALIBRATE

ॐॐॐ

I joined a Phoenix Boy Scout troop, and my scoutmaster, Alan, provided a strong father role model for me. His manliness and integrity inspired me and helped me achieve the highest rank available — that of Eagle Scout. Although I enjoyed the scouting activities for the most part, I was pretty much on my own. I just kept pushing ahead, one day at a time.

"Would you like to come with me to hear a speaker?" my friend David asked when I was a senior in high school. I went just to be with my Boy Scout friends and to see what was going on.

The speaker gave a lot of interesting facts that I'd never heard — like in Europe, if you dig far down enough, you hit sand and that this indicated there had been some kind of catastrophic flood.

"Also, dinosaur bone fields have been uncovered all over the world, which proves that these dinosaurs died suddenly and cataclysmically. Hundreds of ancient cultures, from Hawaii to Mexico to Japan, contain stories in ancient folklore about a massive flood that once covered the earth with only a single family surviving."

He told us how eons ago, God called a man named Noah to build a type of boat called an ark and that when this huge ark was complete, God flooded the entire earth and destroyed everything and everyone not in the ark and started all over again.

PUSHING THROUGH

This piqued my interest. I became interested in learning about God and began going to church.

ॐॐॐ

As I grew older, I needed to work to buy my own clothes and books. My job at the local grocery store paid minimum wage — 75 cents per hour. After months of working in the produce section, I thought, *I've got to concentrate on a real future, and it's not going to happen on this job. What can I do?* My friend and I had joined the Coast Guard Reserves when I was 17, and he'd gone on to active duty. *Maybe I'll do the same. I'd gain usable skills and serve my country as well.*

I visited a recruiting office in downtown Phoenix to enlist. The Coast Guard sent me to Alameda, California, for Basic Training, where we enjoyed a stunning view of Alcatraz.

After boot camp, the Coast Guard assigned me to a search and rescue vessel from San Pedro, California. On board, I served as quartermaster and thoroughly enjoyed the excitement and challenge of rescuing boaters in distress and patrolling the coastal waters.

While at sea, we all worked four hours on, four off. Within a few months, I qualified for training in electronics and was transferred to a base in Connecticut. I decided to become a career guardsman.

"What will you do on your Christmas leave?" a fellow guardsman asked. "Go home to Arizona?"

RECALIBRATE

"No, I think I'll go back to Iowa and visit my aunt. I've not seen her for some time."

"Stay warm," he said, laughing.

❧❧❧

I enjoyed a close relationship with God through his son, Jesus, after I heard that speaker when I was in Boy Scouts. *God, I want to belong to you. I want purpose in life. I want to know that you put me on the planet for a reason.*

On Christmas morning, I walked down the street to attended services at the local church. When the collection basket came around, I put my meager dollar in and silently said to God, *I am your servant, do with me what you want.*

❧❧❧

Where am I? My head felt as heavy as an anchor and pounded as hard as the seas in a storm. I forced my eyes open and saw Mom sitting next to me. *Mom? What are you doing here?*

"Keep still," she said. "Don't try to move."

"Wha …"

"Shhh. You are in the hospital."

"Why?" My tongue felt like I'd sucked on sea kelp.

She laid a hand on mine. "You had an accident. On the boat."

"How?"

"Apparently you lost your balance. You fell from the second deck to the first."

"I can't move." Panic rose up like brackish bile in my throat.

"Try to keep still, John. You landed on your head in the fall. The doctors had to perform emergency surgery. Please, try to relax."

"When?"

"Six weeks ago."

"*Six weeks?* Are you serious?" I squeezed my eyes shut and took a deep breath. "How bad was I hurt?"

She glanced away. "I'll let the doctor explain."

"What is going on?" I asked the doctor when he came in. "Give it to me straight."

"You have suffered extensive brain trauma," he said. "When you fell on your head, some of your brain protruded from its sac. We had to remove that part of your brain. It has affected your gross motor skills and how your mind functions."

I had to let the words slowly sink in. I found out I was in the general hospital in Hartford, Connecticut. The left side of my body was paralyzed. My right eye drooped almost shut, and my left field of vision was gone from both eyes.

As difficult as it was, I resolved to just accept the situation and make the most of it because I'd learned early in life that you just push on even when things get tough. But I knew I couldn't do it alone. *I sure didn't expect this when I told God he could do anything he wanted with me!*

I wondered, *How will he help me out of this situation?*

A nurse came in and said, "We're transferring you to a military hospital in Massachusetts for recovery and rehabilitation. You will receive intensive physical therapy there." They rolled me out to the ambulance. I lay helpless on the stretcher. During the next six months of hospitalization, I kept hearing those words in my head, "You'll never walk again."

The grueling physical therapy stretched my strength and willpower to the limit while I struggled to compensate for my limitations — getting dressed one-handed, taking care of personal hygiene and keeping my balance. Simply putting one foot in front of the other took all my energy, but the determination to walk again propelled me forward.

"I WILL walk out of here!" I told a nurse.

She smiled, her eyes filled with pity as she touched my shoulder.

You'll see. I kept my thoughts to myself. I put my trust in what I had read in the Bible, that "with Christ all things are possible" (Philippians 4:13). *I will walk again because I believe God's word over the doctor's.* I prayed all the time and trusted God to restore my ability to walk and take care of myself.

The head injury also caused memory and cognitive impairment, which made it tough to read, write or think clearly. Retraining my mind proved just as challenging as retraining my body, but six months after I entered the rehabilitation hospital — helpless — I *walked* out with Christ's help, just as I had promised that nurse.

PUSHING THROUGH

In spite of my accomplishment, the doctors released me with their official diagnosis: *Feebleminded.* I wondered if I'd really be mentally challenged all my life. The Coast Guard supplied me with a fellow guardsman to escort me back home to Arizona where I continued my struggle toward normalcy.

I gradually regained the ability to reason and take care of myself.

❧❧❧

Now what can I do? I pondered the problem two years later. Although once again able to walk, my whole left side remained weak. *Perhaps I should go back to school and trust God to restore all my mental faculties,* I thought. I enrolled at the local community college, working harder and longer than most students likely had to as I struggled to overcome my physical and mental impairments. I tired easily and found it hard to focus, but I pressed on, knowing and believing in Christ's help. *God didn't create me and save my life to sit around and stagnate. He'll help me get a degree.*

I worked toward my goals with tenacity and faith that God is good, no matter what.

After achieving an associate's degree, I set my sights on the next goal — a bachelor's at Arizona State University. *I'd like to teach high school math.*

The Coast Guard had awarded me full medical discharge and granted me a small pension. Then, the GI

RECALIBRATE

Bill was passed into law and provided funding for education. With those small amounts of money, I managed to live on my own while attending the university. Again, I worked harder and longer than others seemed to need to but finally achieved my degree and teacher certification. Shortly after graduation, I landed a job teaching math at a local high school.

࿎࿎࿎

"My name is Mr. VanDruff," I addressed the class on the first day. I explained to the students that I had vision impairment, but it did not keep me from seeing the knowledge and beauty of mathematics that I wanted to share with them.

Plus, I saw this as an opportunity to model what I believed about overcoming challenges.

Teaching high school kids proved enjoyable. I loved the kids but cared little for the politics of administration or parents who tried to get me to change grades so their Charlie could play on the football team or Suzie could keep her perfect 4.0 average.

While teaching, I decided to pursue more education. Once I'd achieved my master's, I searched for another job.

I saw an ad on the jobs board at ASU that intrigued me. A teaching position at a university in Tacoma, Washington. I'd never liked the heat of the Southwest and figured this job could be a great option, so I applied.

I got the job and settled into the life, beauty and gentle rain of the Puget Sound region. I worked one year at the university before moving on to another local college where I spent the next three decades. During the summers, I traveled back to Arizona State University to complete my doctorate in math education.

৵৵৵

I married and had two children. Our marriage was difficult, but having my daughter and son strengthened my resolve to make the marriage work. *I won't put my kids through a divorce. I know what it's like and can't do that to them.*

৵৵৵

My wife flew back to Arizona to help her parents celebrate their 50th wedding anniversary, while I stayed home with our kids. My son, then 17, suffered from severe asthma and awakened me most mornings with persistent coughing. One morning, he sounded different. I heard gurgling sounds.

I rushed to his bedroom and shook his shoulders. "Wake up!"

No response. I dashed to the phone and dialed 911.

"I'm sorry," the emergency room doctor later said. "Your son didn't make it."

"What? Why?" I sat down hard.

"Combination of heart virus with the asthma. I'm so sorry," he repeated.

I was devastated. *How could a good God take my son?*

RECALIBRATE

I was so angry that I turned away from him as I tried to make sense of it all.

Only a person who's lost a child can understand the lingering pain I endured for many years. My son's death was an unexpected challenge, but in the end, I made up my mind not to let it destroy me.

తతత

Our marriage flat-lined after our son's death, but I refused to quit. *I promised before God and man till death do us part.*

I did quit on God, though. I could take the challenges of my own injuries after the accident — which I felt he allowed to happen exactly five weeks after I again gave him my life and told him that he could do whatever he wanted with me. I believed God proved his love through all the rehabilitation. I believed he had helped me to walk again and to become an educated man with a good career.

But my son's death?

God, this is too much.

తతత

Zero plus zero equals zero. The thought popped into my head as I graded math papers. *Zero matter plus zero matter will always equal zero.* My hands shook as I laid the red pencil on my desk. *Somehow, I know that you still love me, even though I gave up on you, God, and went back on my promise to you. I'm so very, very sorry, God.*

PUSHING THROUGH

You can do with me whatever you want, and I will always love and trust you.

ᔑᔑᔑ

Our marriage didn't work out. We divorced.

Lonely, I found a Web site for Christian singles in August of 2005 and submitted a short bio. A few days later, I got a response.

"Hi, I'm Betty. I read your bio. We have a lot of similar interests."

"Hi, Betty, what might those interests be?" We corresponded over the Web site.

"For starters, we both have our doctorates in education. We're both retired, although I still do research, teach part time at the university and lead professional development seminars."

I learned Betty had been widowed 10 years and lived in Missouri.

"I love the Pacific Northwest," she wrote. "My sister lives there, and I have visited many times. I love it there because it's so green and pretty."

God, I feel like I've met a woman who loves you as much as I do, I prayed after another conversation with her. I felt our spirits and souls were on the same plane and wondered if it was possible for me to experience true love with her.

"I would love to meet you," I told Betty three months after our first contact. "Will you let me buy you a ticket to fly out here?"

"I'd love that!"

I purchased a first-class seat. When the day arrived, I took my hand-lettered sign with her name and headed for Sea-Tac Airport.

I watched all the passengers flow past me from Betty's plane. No Betty. I fought to still the trembling in my hands as I held the sign.

"Hi, I'm Betty." A smiling lady approached. "Sorry I'm late. I stopped in the ladies room."

We hugged and I said, "At some point, we need to pray about this relationship."

"How about now?" she replied and reached for my hand.

"Of course," I said. "Now is perfect. God," I prayed, "we ask your blessing and guidance on this relationship."

"Amen." Betty squeezed my hand.

We collected her bags and boarded a minibus from the airport to Gig Harbor. I felt like a schoolboy as I leaned in to kiss her. We kissed and kissed. Only our arrival in Gig Harbor ended the embrace. Before we got to my house, we both agreed we were meant to be together. At 69 years old, God gave me my soul mate.

"I want to meet your family," I said as her visit came to an end. "Let's check the Internet for flights and see what we can find."

"How about coming for Thanksgiving?" Betty suggested. "You'll get to meet lots of family then."

"Okay, I will. That sounds like a great plan."

Her nephew held an open house, and about 70 people

stopped by. My mind spun at the new names and faces, but the one thing that computed clearly was the love they had for Betty.

"I've already bought a ticket to fly to Texas for my grandson's 1st birthday," Betty told me. "Won't you join me?"

"As your husband?"

"That would be the best gift ever!"

"Then, let's go talk to your pastor."

Betty called and made an appointment.

"We want to be married."

"You'll both have to take a course before I can agree to marry you," he said. He held out a book.

"We'll do it."

We completed the course as we flew from Missouri to Texas together.

"Why don't you just get married there?" Betty's mom suggested when Betty called to tell her we'd arrived safely. "Neither of you are kids. You know what you want."

"Why not?" Betty laughed. "Let's go talk to my son's pastor."

"I'm sorry, but I can't marry you two until you complete a marriage course." He pulled out a book.

We laughed. "We just finished that exact course on the flight down."

"Then, I'll be happy to perform the ceremony." He smiled. "You two are quite inspiring to me! You reflect God's amazing love for us all."

After our Texas celebrate-grandson's-birthday-wedding trip, we returned to St. Louis. We packed up Betty's house for her move to Washington. Then I returned home to Washington, and she flew to Europe to satisfy a six-week commitment of presenting training seminars for educators.

"I can't stand being apart," I moaned two weeks after she left.

"Come on over and join me. We'll tour Europe between conferences."

Since this was my first trip to Europe, everything was new and exciting. When Betty finished her teaching commitment, we returned to the United States and settled into our home in Gig Harbor.

కా కా కా

"I feel we need to find a new church," Betty said three years after our wedding.

"I agree. I want to find a place where we can really mesh."

"Look at this," she said, pointing to the computer screen. "Harbor Life Church. Over on 56th Street. You want to check it out?"

"Sure."

The moment we walked in, we felt the genuine welcome of everyone who met us. They greeted us with warm hugs and smiles.

"God moves with absolute freedom in that church," Betty remarked on the drive home.

"I agree. I feel they don't box him in with man's rules and expectations. Let's go back next Sunday."

Several weeks later, I told Betty, "I feel a real connection with Harbor Life Church."

"Let's make Harbor Life our new church home."

"I'm with you on that."

ಕಾಕಾಕಾ

Two years later, in 2007, I experienced intense pain in my side. "I've got to get to the emergency room and find out what's going on," I told Betty.

The doctor ran tests, including an MRI, and discovered I had kidney stones. The tests also revealed an aneurism in my abdominal aorta.

"You'd have been a goner if we hadn't found that," the doctor said. "You have those painful kidney stones to thank for your survival."

"Actually, I have God to thank," I said.

"Whatever." He smiled. "But, we have to wait until the aneurism is a certain size before we can operate. I need to see you every six months to monitor its growth."

After four years of monitoring, the doctor felt the time had come to operate. He scheduled surgery for May of 2011.

One month before surgery, Betty's mother passed away.

One month after surgery to insert a stent in the aorta, I felt poorly again.

I sat on our bed watching Betty preparing to leave for a weekly Bible study we both attended.

"I think I'll stay home tonight."

"Why?" Betty turned to me in surprise. "You never miss this class."

"I just don't feel well."

"Well, okay, but it won't be the same without you. I'll explain your absence. I'm sure they'll want to pray for you."

Time to empty the dishwasher, I said to myself the next morning. I lowered the lid and picked up a plate. *Plop.* It fell back into the dishwasher.

I picked up a mug. *Plop.* I flexed my fingers several times and tried again. I couldn't keep a grip on anything.

"Maybe I just need to lie down for a little bit."

I staggered down the hall, bumping into the walls like a drunken sailor in a storm.

"Something's seriously wrong," I told Betty. "See if you can get an appointment ASAP."

"Your doctor can see you tomorrow," she told me a little while later.

After a brief exam, the doctor ordered an MRI of my brain. When he saw the results, he made an appointment with a neurologist for 9 a.m. the next day.

By that time, Betty had to ask for a wheelchair to transport me into the office. After reviewing the MRI report, the doctor immediately admitted me to intensive care in the closest hospital. By then, I was so weak I could hardly move. They ran more tests and transported me to the ICU at Harborview Trauma Center in Seattle. There, the medical team identified a number of lesions in my brain. Because they suspected cancer, I was transferred to University of Washington's cancer unit for a biopsy and diagnosis.

"You have cancer in the brain, and it is confirmed as B-cell lymphoma." He tapped the chart in his hand. "I'll give it to you straight. The tumors are malignant, and the situation is fatal if you do nothing. The situation is also fatal if we do anything *wrong*." He sat down and crossed his legs.

"We have to be *very* careful in our approach. The tumors are located in the midbrain region. Impossible to operate. We can't use radiation or you will lose all cognitive ability, and that damage is irreversible. Your only options are different sorts of chemotherapy. I will send an oncologist in to speak to you about those options so you can make the most informed decision possible for this situation."

The doctor walked out. I looked over at Betty, standing by the window. Tears trickled down her cheeks.

I closed my eyes and focused on my vow to God. *I will follow you, no matter what. You can do whatever you want with me.* I remembered how God took me from being told I would never walk to walking, and from being told I would be feebleminded to a doctorate in education.

I recalled how he'd sustained me through my son's death, even when I turned my back on him, and how he'd helped me survive a painful divorce.

Again, I looked over at the woman I'd loved for six years. *And Betty. You gave me Betty. No matter what happens, I know that you are always good.*

I searched for a way to cheer my wife up — to convey to her both my love and God's love for her. I began singing the first words that popped into my mind. "Jesus loves me, this I know, for the Bible tells me so."

She swallowed hard and came over to the bed.

"It will be fine, Betty." I reached for her hand. "God has never failed me yet, and I know he won't this time, either. I have yielded my whole being to him."

The oncologist came in and explained the process of treating the cancer with high-dose chemotherapy. He cautioned that the side effects were going to compromise my immune system and take a toll on my overall health.

By then, I was so weak they had to use a lift to move me. I had no strength, no energy — just dead weight lying in the bed. The chemo began. For six weeks straight, I endured a full day of chemo to attack the cancer, then four to five days of flushing out the poison.

The staff carefully monitored my kidney and liver functions as the toxins streamed through my system. Persistent nausea and headaches made life miserable, but Betty remained at my side day and night, calling the nurse when I was in excessive pain or needed assistance and helping me with my food (when I could eat).

I kept telling myself, *I will not yield to self-pity. Ever. I know Christ will see me through this situation as he has every other challenge of my life.*

PUSHING THROUGH

Even during the chemo treatments, the doctors insisted that I have some physical therapy. It exhausted me, but I was determined to walk *again* because I hated to be pushed in a wheelchair. I graduated to a walker that I called my "stabilizer."

I had flashbacks of those early years in the military hospital. As I did then, I again leaned heavily on the gift of faith that God gave me when I surrendered all to him. Hundreds of friends throughout the country prayed for me on a daily basis. Betty sent out daily emails to update our "prayer partners" on my progress. Our hearts overflowed with thankfulness to be part of a group of people who love and trust the God who answers prayers.

After six weeks in the Cancer Center, the tumors had shrunk to the point where the doctor said we could go home and come back every other week for five days of chemotherapy. I say "we" because cancer does not just affect the one with the disease, it affects all those close to you. In this case, Betty and I walked this journey together. During those long hours in the hospital, we played our favorite card game, SkipBo. My strength gradually returned.

For the following six months, life felt like a pulsating rhythm of the sea — one week at home, one week at the hospital.

Weekly MRIs, then monthly MRIs finally provided the evidence that the tumors were gone. Praise God! I still had my mental capacities, although "chemo brain" sometimes caused me to be a bit foggy.

Finally, with the all-clear report, the oncologist suggested that I go through another round of chemo, something different that should guarantee that the tumors would not return. The only drawback was that this chemo would kill all my bone marrow and immune system. This went against everything I believed about how God designed the immune system to protect the body.

I told the doctor that we would explore other options and came in contact with a naturopathic doctor and naturopathic oncologist at the Seattle Cancer Treatment and Wellness Center in Renton. We began with a few hours of vitamin infusions each week to build up my immune system. After three years of this therapy, I have continued to be cancer-free and function normally as evidenced through bi-annual MRI checkups.

Betty and I clung to God's promises through his word, the Bible. "We know all things work together for good to those who love God" (Romans 8:28) is a favorite, as is Isaiah 40:31: "Those who hope in the Lord will renew their strength. They will soar on wings like eagles. They will run and not grow weary, they will walk and not be faint."

I've decided to live each day to the fullest, trusting God with every moment.

When God chooses to remove me from this life, my heart will echo Paul's words in Philippians 1:21: "For to me, to live is Christ, and to die is gain."

Why? Because earthly death will usher me into the presence of the creator of our amazing universe, and I will finally meet him face to face.

PUSHING THROUGH

Until then, I'm thankful for each day I get to live with my wife and enjoy the company of the people at Harbor Life Church.

CONCLUSION

"Recalculating … recalculating …"

Your GPS is very forgiving. You can head in the wrong direction, yet the GPS will show you how to get back on the right track. How to recalibrate.

Every time we see another person recalibrate, it reminds us that God really loves people and that he is actively pursing us to lead us into a better life. The pain of all the moments gone wrong add up and eventually catch up with us. If you find yourself in that place — tired, confused, off track — know that a moment of hope is not far. It may, however, lie in an unexpected place. And that place is in the embrace of a loving and kind God. This is our invitation to you. Surrender your moments to him.

Change is possible. It's time to recalibrate.

Each of us at Harbor Life Church invites you to come and check out our church community. See if we are for real. Ask questions. Jump in at a pace you are comfortable with. You will find that we are real, authentic and far from perfect. Moments of failure show that we are still in the process of real-life change and that we still need the forgiveness and understanding of others.

If you are unable to check out our church community, but find yourself drawn to recalibrate, I encourage you to consider some basic thoughts.

RECALIBRATE

What is the world like? From cancer and Ebola, to war, terrorism and genocide, most of us don't need to be convinced that something is wrong in our world. No religion in the world deviates from this perspective.

We all ache for a better world. In the same way that hunger points to our need for food and water, the ache we all have inside points to the reality that a better world once existed or one day will exist. From a Christian perspective both are true. A better world once existed and will one day exist again.

The world and everything in it was designed for good. In this better world, we were designed to put the needs of others before our own and to care for each other. We also were designed to take care of the world as God took care of us. We were designed to be content with God, with ourselves and with others.

Our world has been damaged by evil. The problems of the world we live in reflect the shift that took place in humanity. We became discontent with God and wanted to do things our way and independent of him. We failed to take care of each other, and we put our own needs before the needs of others. We wanted to be independent of God and his influence. There are consequences to such thinking and behavior. As a result, our world is damaged by evil.

CONCLUSION

Introduced to a better way to live. God loved us and the planet too much to leave us in our own brokenness. His response to our brokenness may surprise you. God came into our world of brokenness as a human, Jesus, and began to teach us that there is a better way to live. The good that is supposed to happen in our world can happen as we identify with Jesus and his teachings — as our hearts change toward him, the world and others.

Restored for better. Jesus with his life, death and resurrection did what no other human could do. He made a way for a world damaged by evil to be restored for better. Jesus lived a perfect life and was nailed to a tree an innocent man to provide a way toward a better world. A new beginning is made possible because of Jesus. In this, God demonstrated his great love for us.

Jesus started a revolution. We need Jesus to become the good we want to be in the world. As he heals us, we get to then play a part in the healing of others and in showing the world that there is a better way to live. This is the life that Jesus invites us to be part of, and it's why he pursues us.

"For God so loved the world that he gave his only son, so that everyone who believes in him may not perish but may have eternal life. Indeed, God did not send the son into the world to condemn the world, but in order that the world might be saved through him" (John 3:16,17).

RECALIBRATE

Join the revolution. Are you ready to follow Jesus? Take a step or leap of faith and invite him into your life. Acknowledge your need for him and take steps toward him by reading the Bible, communicating with him in prayer and by getting connected with a community of Christ followers.

We invite you to visit us at Harbor Life Church. We'd love to meet you!

Pastor Tyson Lash
Harbor Life Church
Gig Harbor, Washington

Join others who are still in the process of recalibrating their lives.

Harbor Life Church
4417 56th Street NW
Gig Harbor, WA 98335

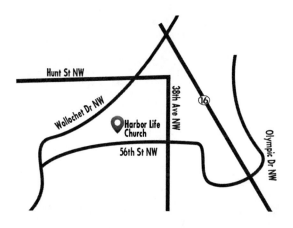

Service Times: Sundays at 9 and 10:45 a.m.

Phone: 253.851.1734
Web site: www.theharborlife.com
Email: info@theharborlife.com

Dress is casual, so come as you are. Our first gathering (9 a.m.) is about 65 minutes in length, and the second gathering (10:45 a.m.) is a little more fluid and about 75 minutes in length. The music is inspiring, the people real and the talks meaningful.

Making Our World A Better Place